Euro on Trial

Also by Brendan Brown

THE DOLLAR–MARK AXIS
MONETARY CHAOS IN EUROPE 1914–31
THE FLIGHT OF INTERNATIONAL CAPITAL 1931–86
ECONOMISTS AND FINANCIAL MARKETS
THE YO-YO YEN

Euro on Trial

To reform or split up?

Brendan Brown

First published 2004 by
PALGRAVE MACMILLAN
Houndmills, Basingstoke, Hampshire RG21 6XS and
175 Fifth Avenue, New York, N.Y. 10010
Companies and representatives throughout the world

PALGRAVE MACMILLAN is the global academic imprint of the Palgrave
Macmillan division of St. Martin's Press, LLC and of Palgrave Macmillan Ltd.
Macmillan® is a registered trademark in the United States, United Kingdom
and other countries. Palgrave is a registered trademark in the European
Union and other countries.

ISBN 1–4039–1284–X

This book is printed on paper suitable for recycling and made from fully
managed and sustained forest sources.

A catalogue record for this book is available from the British Library.

Library of Congress Cataloging-in-Publication Data
    Brown, Brendan, 1951–
    Euro on trial: to reform or split up?/Brendan Brown.
        p. cm.
    Includes bibliographical references and index.
    ISBN 1–4039–1284–X (cloth)
        1. Monetary unions – European Union countries. 2. Monetary policy –
European Union countries. 3. European Union countries – Economic policy.
4. Economic and Monetary Union. I. Title.
HG3942.B76 2004
332.4'94–dc22   2003066470

10 9 8 7 6 5 4 3 2 1
13 12 11 10 09 08 07 06 05 04

Printed and bound in Great Britain by
Antony Rowe Ltd, Chippenham and Eastbourne

Contents

List of Cartoons

Acknowledgements

I acknowledge the gracious offer of the cartoonists, Patrick Chappatte and Rainer Hachfeld, to help me provide contemporary artistic illustrations of the journey towards European Monetary Union. They both supplied me with a wide assortment of relevant works, from which I chose the representations included here. Grateful acknowledgement is also made to Pierre Reymond for permission to use his cartoon 'Giscard and Schmidt' which appeared in *Sédition Speciale* (Geneva: Tribune de Genève, 1979).

BRENDAN BROWN

1
The Hidden Alternative

Was the launch of the euro an expensive and dangerous mistake for the peoples of Europe? If so, who was to blame? And what are the escape routes – either in the form of bold reform or of break-up? These questions – and the responses – form the substance of the present volume. Only the last question – and the attempt to answer it by drafting detailed scenarios in which present member countries could exit from monetary union – is new. The potential costs and benefits and the motives or competence of the policy-makers had been extensively debated in the roughly three decades up until the realization of European Monetary Union (EMU) in 1999.

The justification for re-posing the same questions and adding the third concerning reversibility of monetary union lies partly in the new evidence now available from several years of experience. President Mitterrand used to say that one had to give time to Time. Five years on from the launch of the euro new interpretations are possible of the actors, forces, and events that together brought the euro into existence. Some flaws are already apparent in the architecture. A serious reform of the union – if indeed it could be implemented – would increase its power of survival. But it is more than a remote possibility that the one-time visionary statesmen who believed their monetary creation to be irreversible and a guarantor of permanent tranquillity in Europe will suffer the fate of Ozymandias within a generation.

A starting-point in judging the euro enterprise is to examine critically the promises of a better future made by its promoters and advocates. How do the various prospectuses read today in the light of experience and of further intellectual reflection? And how insightful were the criticisms of EMU made by its opponents in the hope of bringing the euro train to a halt before reaching its destination? Were there failings in the various democratic checks and balances that allowed such a dangerous and costly journey to continue?

There was no menu of monetary choice on display. Jacques Delors once quipped that a married man is not forbidden from looking at beautiful women any more than a person on a diet from looking at the dinner menu. But when it came to the new monetary regime being imposed on Europe by the troika of Helmut Kohl, François Mitterrand, and Jacques Delors, European citizens, including parliamentarians, were not able to view a well-presented selection of different possible currency arrangements.

A European monetary menu

What would a European monetary menu have looked like? There would have been four main choices, including first, the monetary union under construction. This first choice consisted of a supranational money for all the countries in the European Community (subsequently renamed European Union) which would replace all existing national monies. A federal institution, the European Central Bank (ECB) would be responsible for the conduct of monetary policy. The ECB would exercise its authority with total independence from member governments but within a constitutional framework as specified by an EU treaty.

The second possibility was a universal free float, with exchange rates between each of the national monies in the EU being determined without official intervention in the currency markets. A system of co-operation would have been developed with the aim of limiting potential monetary disturbances which any one country might cause with respect to the other highly interdependent economies. The large central banks (able to emit the most damaging shocks on their neighbours) – the Bundesbank and Banque de France in particular – might have bound themselves to some surveillance or even external policing (by, say, a European Monetary Authority) with respect to their setting of inflation targets. And to underpin transparency and mutual trust, the policy-making councils of the large national central banks might have included central bankers from other European countries (for example, the Bundesbank Council could have included a Banque de France council member).

Third, Europe's monetary order could be based round one anchor currency. The central bank of the anchor currency would set monetary policy, based primarily on its target for price level stability in its own political jurisdiction. But some flexibility would be possible so that in extreme circumstances conditions in other EU countries would provide grounds for tolerating some deviation from target even over the medium term. All non-anchor countries in the EU would run monetary policies based on achieving stability of the exchange rate between their own and the anchor currency. ('Stability' is subject to wide interpretation. If the exchange rate swings within large bands which are adjusted frequently, then the anchor-based system is not very different from the freely floating system, the first item on the menu.)

In practice, the Deutschmark was the anchor in just such a system during the decade that ended with the launch of the euro. (No change occurred in the key Deutschmark–French franc parity and any significant market fluctuations around that were only short-lived – on two occasions as much as 5 per cent for a few weeks.) There was a fleeting proposal (made by Paris during the currency crisis of July 1993) for the French franc to become a second anchor, itself floating freely against the Deutschmark, and having a group of currencies pegged to it. But both geographic and historical considerations suggest that such a twin anchor system would have been infeasible. In particular, the Netherlands, Belgium, and Austria out of economic and political considerations would always choose the Deutschmark rather than the French franc as anchor. Spain and Italy would rather tie their currencies to a large Deutschmark zone than to the lone French franc.

The fourth choice would have been a hybrid regime. Some EU countries, including the hitherto anchor currency country (Germany), could join together in monetary union. Other EU countries would either adopt the new money as their anchor or allow their own money to float freely. Within the freely floating system, explicit monetary co-operation (in the setting of inflation targets and other aspects of policy) might have evolved on a bilateral rather than EU-wide basis. Or monetary union might have emerged on a regional basis not including the anchor currency – in particular the Belgian franc, Dutch guilder, and Luxembourg franc might have merged into a new common currency for the 'Low Countries' which would have floated freely versus the French franc and Deutschmark.

In search of a replacement for the Deutschmark anchor

In reviewing the arguments made for European Monetary Union, the dominant theme was how the new regime would be an improvement both from an economic and political perspective on the Deutschmark-anchored system then in force. The hypothetical alternative of a freely floating exchange rate system in Europe, fortified by monetary co-operation, was never seriously explored at the level of public discourse. The key discussions were of course between France and Germany – the twin drivers of the monetary union train. The destination could not be reached without both French and German governments being fully on board. It was not crucial to the enterprise whether other governments were on or off.

The interest of the French policy-making elite in European Monetary Union grew largely out of anxiety about German monetary power. This can be traced back as far as November 1968, when Bonn virtually demanded that Paris devalue the franc so as to diffuse a European monetary crisis in the wake of the French social and labour turmoil earlier in the year. The growing international role of the Deutschmark (which coincided with falling confidence in the stability of the US dollar) seemed to be translating itself into growing power and even hegemony on the European stage for Germany. This fear of German financial and possible future political might did not rest on economic growth data. During the last three decades of the twentieth century cumulative growth in France and Germany was virtually identical – albeit with periods of some years when the differential was persistently in favour of one or the other. And though unification brought a once-and-for all increase in German economic size it was also a source of weakness.

According to the dominant prescription of French policy-makers, the way to contain nascent German power was to tie the Deutschmark and Bundesbank into a European monetary union. (The exact form of that union – and whether for example national currencies would continue to exist alongside a common European one – remained somewhat vague right up until the early 1990s.) In broader terms, Paris was concerned throughout, albeit at varying degrees, by the possibility that Germany might go it alone as the largest European economy, and reach direct bilateral alliances with Russia (Soviet Union) and the USA. Monetary union could be a means of locking Germany into a European 'confederation' over which Paris might hope to have dominance as regards foreign policy issues, given its veto power at the UN Security Council and its independent nuclear deterrent. French policy-makers failed to understand that a badly constructed union might indeed eclipse the Bundesbank but at the cost of imposing on France and Germany a flawed monetary regime administered by ivory-tower central bankers.

German policy-makers were of course fully aware of the French reasons for pressing ahead with monetary union. Indeed, these came fully into the open during the French referendum in autumn 1992 on the

Maastricht Treaty, when many of the politicians prominent in the Yes campaign, including the prime minister, Pierre Bérégovoy, roused voters by arguing that rejection could mean a rebirth of German nationalism. (In fact Bérégovoy was no fan of monetary union, as we shall see in Chapter 2.) In general, Bonn (and later Berlin) embraced the potential of monetary union to act as a barrier against dark nationalistic forces from within ever swaying the Federal Republic away from integration into Western Europe and towards dangerous 'go alone' alliances and adventurism. But the German enthusiasts of West European integration wanted a deeper political dimension than Paris – not a committee of foreign ministers under the dominance of Paris but a supranational political system (including a European parliament with considerable authority and an elected president). Political union in Europe was the prize. If this could be had without monetary sacrifice, that would be the best of all worlds, allowing the Deutschmark (the most popular creation of the Federal Republic) to be saved. But certain concessions might have to be made to the French viewpoint (on monetary union) in the bargaining process.

Some German statesmen (in particular, Helmut Schmidt and Hans-Dietrich Genscher) had serious reservations in any case about the status quo of the Deutschmark. The wielding of power by the Bundesbank *vis-à-vis* other European nations, and in particular *vis-à-vis* France, was seen as putting damaging strains on European integration in other areas. Some saw Deutschmark nationalism as objectionable in itself, given Germany's past. Helmut Schmidt, as chancellor, had dwelt on the legacy of Auschwitz in an address to the Bundesbank Council in November 1978, when pleading the case for the European Monetary System then being set up (see Marsh, 1992).

Schmidt also was amongst those who argued that the Deutschmark's grown international role meant the German economy was dangerously exposed to global capital flows which otherwise might have been diluted across the wide span of all EU countries. In principle, though, that particular disadvantage could be reduced by the French franc assuming a greater international investment role, meaning that the periodic shift in momentum of capital flows across the Atlantic would impact both the franc and the mark rather than being concentrated on the mark.

The EMU enthusiasts in Paris and Bonn had a different idea. US monetary and fiscal shocks had been a source of considerable turbulence for the European economy as a whole and it would better resist them if joined together in monetary union with a currency which rivalled the

1   The euro as seen by ...

Source: Chappatte, *Die Weltwoche*, December 1997.

dollar in international size. The idea was that if a large part of the world used the euro for borrowing, lending, and trade purposes, Europe could gain some insulation from US shock. In practice, though, such rapid progress for the euro was improbable so long as China, Japan, and the Asian region generally would remain in closer interdependence with the US than with Europe. And how big a cushion could a large international role for the euro provide anyhow against US shock? A violent cyclical fluctuation of the US economy would surely pull Europe along in its sweep, with or without the euro.

Claude Trichet, the governor of the Bank of France, had not yet appreciated that point when he made a notoriously bad forecast in January 2001. By then it had become clear that the US economy had entered a severe downturn in the wake of the bursting of the biggest US equity market bubble since 1929. 'It used to be the case that when the USA got a cold, Europe got pneumonia; those days are now over', the governor said. Not only did European Monetary Union fail to prevent pneumonia, but it allowed a particularly virulent strain to take root in the largest member country, Germany.

That is evidence after the fact. Rightly or wrongly, however, there was some consensus (albeit with differing emphasis) amongst important groups of policy-makers (not all) in Paris and Bonn (later Berlin) that monetary integration in Europe would provide insulation against storms from the USA. Events in the late 1980s and early 1990s, in particular German unification, promoted a further consensus view – that integration based on the Deutschmark as anchor was unsustainable in the long run. The stance of monetary policy in the Federal Republic required to restore stability in the wake of an extravagant monetary union between the ex-communist East and West Germany was far tighter than what suited the rest of the European Community.

No monetary anchor would have worked well in such circumstances, but the experience fuelled new resentment amongst Germany's EU partners, particularly France, at the power of the Deutschmark. Simultaneously leading German policy-makers became more ready to sacrifice the Deutschmark with a view to securing the integration of the now larger Federal Republic into the European Community. For Helmut Kohl, as for his mentor, Konrad Adenauer, European union and German union were opposite sides of the same coin. Full participation in the process of monetary union would soothe the anxieties of other European nations about the dangers of a newly united Germany. It was the growing unacceptability of the Deutschmark's anchor role, both from a political and economic perspective, rather than any broad economic argument about the optimum monetary regime in Western Europe, which brought the old monetary regime (European Monetary System) to an end.

In similar fashion it had been the earlier revulsion against the anchor role for the US dollar, rather than economists' arguments about the merits of an alternative international monetary order, which had undermined the Bretton Woods monetary system. Milton Friedman's advocacy of floating exchange rates had about as much (or as little) to do with the birth of the new international monetary system in the early 1970s as Robert Mundell's essays on optimum currency areas with the emergence of European Monetary Union. In the early 1970s the Nixon administration was hell-bent on re-election at any price, whether with inflation or international trade war, or both, and found the old constraints of the dollar's anchor role an anachronism. Germany was not prepared to accept the US lead into higher inflation and preferred to break free from the dollar. France prevaricated, fearing that divorce from the dollar would mean subjugation by the Deutschmark.

French inferiority complex in currency politics

That inferiority complex, characterized by the view that France could not issue a currency of equal or greater quality to that of Germany, remained prevalent in Paris throughout the following three decades. And it was rare for any policy-maker in Germany to confront directly the monetary inferiority complex of his or her French opposite numbers. An exception was the president of the Bundesbank, Karl Otto Pöhl, who in January 1988 commented publicly that the French government should take steps to boost confidence in the franc, 'which could eventually become as attractive as marks for investors' rather than calling for the Bundesbank to provide support.

Throughout the thirty-year period from the disintegration of the dollar-based global fixed-rate exchange rate system (a process which ran for five years from 1968 to 1973) until the launch of the euro (1998–9) there was little serious advocacy in France of promoting the French franc as an independent floating currency which might rival the Deutschmark. The main partial exceptions were Jean-Charles Naouri and Claude Rubinowicz – top advisers to Finance Minister Pierre Bérégovoy in the mid and late 1980s respectively (see Aeschmann, 1999). They pioneered reforms so as to promote Paris as a financial centre and to increase the attractiveness of the French franc to international investors – but under a regime of the franc being firmly anchored to the Deutschmark. There is no evidence that the aim was ever more than to make the franc into a good mark-substitute rather than independent currency. Much earlier, in the 1960s, General de Gaulle and his economic adviser Jacques Rueff had had grand ambitions of turning Paris into a world financial sector and the French franc into a hard currency based on gold, but that was all within the context of a fixed exchange rate system.

Yet a freely floating French franc rivalling the Deutschmark would have been an effective barrier to Germany gaining monetary dominance over France and would have calmed anxiety about Deutschmark nationalism. France would still have had an interest in locking Germany into Europe and maybe gaining some dominance over a joint European foreign policy. And Germany would have had an interest in raising barriers against its dark forces within. The fulfilment of these aims, however, did not require monetary integration.

A free independent franc would have been accompanied most probably by a considerable degree of monetary co-operation between France and Germany. Wild swings in the crucial French franc–Deutschmark rate based on divergent monetary policies could impose serious costs on both economies (French and German) and were best avoided. Costs included an alternating boom–bust cycle in each country's export sector and a beggar-your-neighbour approach to anti-inflation policy. Germany could bring down inflation promptly by pushing the Deutschmark higher against the French franc (and other European currencies). But that would add to short-term inflation pressures in France (and elsewhere in Europe). Conversely, a French strategy of bringing down inflation by pushing up the franc (and triggering parallel appreciation by the Italian lira, for example) could have put upward pressure on German inflation. And in view of the growing interdependence of the economies – stimulated in part by the dismantling of barriers to trade and capital flows – the aim of containing each other's monetary shocks was sure to gain wide approval from the business community in each country.

What was the source of French defeatism and silence on the independent franc alternative? And why was the German side so reluctant, with the partial exception of Bundesbank President Pöhl, to advance it as an alternative to sacrificing the Deutschmark? Some of the explanation doubtless resides in a predilection of German and French policy-makers for exchange rate stability within Europe. Both were convinced that currency instability would be economically harmful. On the French side there were specific concerns that intra-European exchange rate volatility could undermine the Common Agricultural Policy (CAP). Indeed, when Robert Marjolin in the mid-1960s, as a vice-president of the European Commission, made a sketchy first proposal for monetary union, he stressed the benefits in the form of avoiding frictions in the CAP.

On the German side there was considerable suspicion that currency independence would be used to engineer a competitive advantage for French industry. The plunge of the French franc in the mid-1970s and again in the early 1980s had taken a serious toll at the time on the German export sector and left deep suspicions about Paris's use of the currency tool. German industrial lobbies were strongly in favour of tying the franc–mark rate, rather than leaving it floating and thereby subject to manipulation for competitive purposes. The same lobbies also canvassed Bonn for a fixed exchange rate system which would limit competitive devaluations by Italy.

If indeed a fixed exchange rate system were to be constructed in Western Europe, then it would be hard to imagine it being based on the French franc as anchor. Economic geography was against the French franc. The West German economy was somewhat larger than the French. But more important than that, West Germany was surrounded by smaller countries (Holland, Belgium, Luxembourg, Austria, Denmark, Switzerland) for whom Germany rather than France was the dominant trade partner. These countries had a natural interest in some degree of stability for their own currencies versus the Deutschmark. In addition, from the early 1980s onwards, Holland had opted virtually to join the German monetary zone, adding to its relative size advantage over France. The Deutschmark was the apparent anchor currency – so long as German inflation performance was at least as good as French. In reality, of course, German inflation performance was substantially superior through the 1970s and first half of the 1980s, bestowing an even greater advantage on the Deutschmark as potential (and actual) anchor.

France did break from the Deutschmark anchor at various times – specifically when the French franc was temporarily pulled out of the Snake in early 1974 and again in 1976. (The Snake was an early version of the European Monetary System in which members stabilized their currencies within narrow margins of a Deutschmark parity.) But these pull-outs were forced by massive speculation against existing parities rather than representing the deliberate choice by a French government to launch a reputable independent monetary policy that would allow a freely floating franc to thrive. Indeed, the dominant theme of French monetary history in the period 1973–83 is a refusal to launch the all-out monetary attack on inflation such as the Bundesbank had organized in 1973–4, the Federal Reserve under Paul Volcker later in 1979–82, and the Thatcher government in 1979–81. French monetary policy-makers (including, crucially, Prime Minister Raymond Barre from 1976 to 1981), like the Federal Reserve under Arthur Burns (1970–7), decided that the high inflation, which had emerged during the fantastic boom, and, finally, oil price explosion of the early 1970s, should be tackled by a policy of gradualism. They rejected the policy option of a gung-ho money squeeze of unprecedented severity. The decision doubtless owed much to political calculation. In France there was a steady run of close electoral contests (from the mid-1970s until 1981) between the ruling (yet in-fighting) right-wing parties and the Mitterrand-led alliance of the communists and socialists. Gradualism – and its failure – ruled out any role for the French franc as a competitor of the Deutschmark.

When Jacques Delors as French finance minister in early 1983 embarked on a new austerity programme which eventually helped to bring inflation down to German levels, it was not as part of a game-plan to belatedly launch an independent French franc. His crackdown featured budget cutbacks – reversing and blocking any further implementation of the joint programme agreed between the socialists and communists (whose alliance had been victorious in the presidential and legislative elections of spring 1981) – and a severe incomes policy. These unpopular measures were driven by the slogan of preventing a further devaluation of the French franc against the Deutschmark – in effect making France a dependable member of a DM-anchored European monetary system.

Suppose French stabilization in the early to mid-1980s had come in the fashion of earlier German (1973–5), US (1979–82), or indeed British (1979–82) anti-inflation policies – a big monetary squeeze with the national currency racing to spectacularly high levels, to fall back subsequently when the goal of low inflation was secured. Could this have been a springboard to the French franc becoming a middle-ranking freely floating international investment money (similar to the role played by the British pound since the Thatcher stabilization)? Most probably yes. The Deutschmark would still probably have been ahead of the French franc in terms of international investor market share – but how far ahead is open to question. A previously inexperienced tendency of the Deutschmark to depreciate in the late 1990s and early 2000s might well have given the French franc a crucial boost in the popularity stakes.

Duisenberg's monetary defeatism bolstered German hegemony

A freely floating, or at least partially independent, Dutch guilder would have been crucial to the French franc gaining equality with the Deutschmark and to the erosion of German monetary hegemony in Europe. If the Dutch guilder had been made at least partially independent of the Deutschmark, most probably the Belgian franc also would have floated. Political considerations would have argued against Brussels accepting a lone satellite role to Germany. (Historically the Flemish population in Belgium have been inclined to follow the Dutch example on currency policy, and the Walloon population the French example.) By contrast, with Holland in virtual monetary union with Germany, the sheer size of the greater Deutschmark area meant that German monetary conditions had more influence on France and other European economies than conversely. Moreover, the Deutschmark markets were typically somewhat deeper and more liquid than those in French francs on account of their economic size.

In practice, the Dutch central bank under Wilhelm Duisenberg from 1983 onwards became totally committed to strict Deutschmark zone membership. President Duisenberg gained the nickname in Paris of 'Mr Five Minutes' for the rapidity with which the Dutch central bank followed each and every interest rate decision of the Bundesbank. And so most likely the Deutschmark would have remained as number one European currency even if the French franc had successfully emerged as a quality independent money in the wake of a Volcker-type attack on inflation. But the fact that an independent French franc would be somewhat below the Deutschmark in the international size scales was hardly relevant to French policy-makers in any hypothetical decision as regards their country's future currency policy.

In fact, the only evidence of the independent option being considered at all relates to the beginning of 1983 when President Mitterrand was entertaining 'visitors in the night' who proposed pulling the French franc out of the European Monetary System so that the Socialist policy-programme could be salvaged. In principle the Mitterrand administration could have run larger budget deficits swollen by increased social expenditures, accompanied this with a strict monetary policy so as to bring inflation down sharply, and allowed any flight of capital driven by fears of higher taxation to pull the franc to a cheap level. The erosion of domestic investment opportunity and inflamed perceptions of business risk due to implementation of socialist policies could have been offset (in terms of their drag on the economy) by the franc being at a cheap enough level to generate attractive profit margins in the traded goods and services sector (export and import-competing industries).

In practice, Jacques Delors as finance minister did not have his heart in salvaging socialism, and the administration's economic advisers did not come up with a proposal which would have made this possible. François Mitterrand did request Laurent Fabius, then the budget minister and a member of the president's inner circle (unlike Delors), to present an alternative policy to the Deutschmark satellite one being proposed by Delors. Fabius and Bérégovoy, then chief of staff at the Elysee and subsequently minister of finance, were both advocates at that time of pulling the French franc out of the ERM. But Fabius took advice from Michel Camdessus, the then top official amongst France's economic policy elite (subsequently to become head of the Bank of France and then of the IMF), who advised him that any other course than anchoring to the Deutschmark would lead to national bankruptcy. The idea that France, one of the richest countries in the world, with a budget deficit of only 3 per cent of GDP, was at risk of bankruptcy smacks of alarmism used to justify an entrenched policy preference rather than of sound analysis. Camdessus certainly earned his place at the January 1999 celebratory lunch in Paris to which all leading French politicians and civil servants instrumental in driving EMU forward were invited. But the prince who chooses a bad counsellor gets the advice he deserves ...

Historical accounts suggest that François Mitterrand had his own reasons, in any event, for rejecting the independent alternative. In particular, he had already decided on the new mission for his presidency of advancing European integration, with France taking a lead role together with Germany in the process. With the nomination of Jacques Delors as president of the EU Commission the following year (1984), there was no turning back to reflect on independent monetary options for France. Instead, consensus Euro-thinking on the economics of money became the unquestioned backdrop to French policy-making. Euro-thinking, as evidenced by publications out of the EU Commission during the late 1980s and early 1990s (under Jacques Delors as its president from 1985 to 1994), gave considerable weight to economic gains from reduction and eventual elimination of exchange risk between the European currencies. The Single Market programme (launched by the Single Market Act of 1987 and to be complete by 1992) depended for its success (according to the Brussels propaganda machine) on monetary integration.

Optimum currency area theory misapplied by Brussels

The theory of optimum currency areas (which identifies the costs and benefits of a country or region having its own currency as against joining in the use of a larger one) played some considerable part in the development of the Brussels case, even though some economists used it more persuasively as an argument against monetary union in Western Europe (see, for example, Feldstein, 1997). Also implicit in Euro-thinking was a growing monetary nihilism – the idea that monetary policy could achieve little once inflation was indeed tamed, and that structural policies at a national level would have to be implemented as integration progressed. As we shall see, some key national policy-makers, particularly in Paris, welcomed the idea of European monetary union becoming a backdoor way of forcing the pace on wider institutional (sometimes described as 'structural economic') reform.

The economics-based case of the monetary integrationists (otherwise described as advocates of monetary union) was by no means compelling, and the point has been widely made that the train to European Monetary Union would not have travelled far on what fuel could be provided from economic debate. Indeed, many leading independent economists, especially in the USA (including Milton Friedman, Martin Feldstein, Paul Krugman), but also in Germany, were hostile. In France the picture was more mixed due to the lack of independence in the economic profession and even where research institutes enjoyed nominal independence their dependence on government contracts raised conflicts of interest.

The passage of time has eroded further the economics-based case for monetary union. For example, two West European countries, the UK and Switzerland, which have remained outside the European Monetary Union and maintained fully independent monetary policies, have not suffered any obvious economic handicap as a result. On several measures they have outperformed the euro-area. In North America, the Canadian economy has thrived from a heightened economic integration with the USA (under the North American Free Trade Act 1993) without the construction of a currency union and whilst continuing to maintain a fully independent currency. The laboratory of experience does not confirm the hypothesis that suppression of exchange risk is essential to the flourishing of economic union (the UK and Switzerland are in economic union with the euro-area, Canada in near economic union with the USA).

Indeed, it is quite possible in theory for an economic union (defined by absence of barriers – regulatory or otherwise – to free movement of goods, services, labour, and capital) to include more than one so-called optimum currency area. For obvious reasons this point never formed part of the analyses presented by economists in or near the Brussels propaganda machine. Mundell's original discussion of optimum currency area theory was in the context of North America, where hypothetically the West of Canada and of the USA was specialized in the lumber industry and the East of both countries in manufacturing. Under certain conditions (including low level of labour mobility between East and West), Mundell suggested that there could be economic gain from creating one currency for the West (of the USA and Canada) and one for the East. Then adjustments in each region to economic shocks affecting that region only could occur more rapidly and flexibly with less loss of output. Currency boundaries would divide North America into West and East rather than coinciding with political boundaries. But both West and East would remain in full economic union.

Optimum currency area theory has developed far from Mundell's original contribution. But a persistent theme is the idea that if two countries are subject to considerable risk of asymmetric economic shocks and labour is not highly mobile between the two, then a monetary union between them would have on balance negative economic consequences. On the other hand, smallness and openness are properties which in principle favour monetary union, for a small money is inherently less useful than a large, and openness means that there would be considerable instability in the domestic price level as a consequence of exchange rate fluctuations. Judgement on the optimality of monetary union involves a trade-off between the costs of losing one degree of freedom in adapting to economic shock and gaining the benefits of a large and high-quality money.

The advocates of monetary union argue that likely shocks to the various European economies are symmetric rather than asymmetric, given their highly diversified industrial structure. Asymmetric shocks in the past were largely related (according to the advocates) to independent monetary or fiscal action. But in a monetary union with supranational limits on fiscal policy these would no longer occur. Moreover, in the open European economies the costs of exchange rate adjustment in response to what asymmetric shocks did occur were not evidently less than the costs of relative overall price level adjustment between countries in a monetary union.

As illustration of this last point, suppose an asymmetric shock (such as a collapse of the German real estate market) means that the real exchange rate of the Deutschmark should fall by 5 per cent versus the French franc. In principle this could come about via a 5 per cent devaluation of the Deutschmark with no change in the German or French price level, or by the price level in Germany falling by 5 per cent relative to in France, and no change in the nominal exchange rate. The opponents of union would say that the devaluation alternative was the simplest and least costly, especially if there were no inflation in France (for then, in the absence of exchange-rate change, the price level in Germany must actually fall, rather than simply rising by less than in France). Milton Friedman argued, in his classic essay on floating exchange rates, that it is simpler to turn the clock back one hour – adjust the currency down – than require everyone to wake up an hour sooner – cut wages and prices. The advocates of union argue that the devaluation of the mark would set off a wage–price spiral in Germany – as prices rose and wage-earners sought compensation – and erode confidence in monetary stability over the longer term.

Real estate market bubbles undermine monetary union

The case for European countries preserving independent monies and the possibility of exchange rate adjustment starts with the observation that asymmetric shocks are a more serious consideration than the advocates of monetary union would make us believe. The textbook literature on optimum currency areas makes use of simplistic illustrations such as Germany producing sausages and France cheese and a shift in demand between the two commodities. These are of limited relevance to the advanced industrial economies in Western Europe and the advocates of EMU had little trouble in making light of them. The literature is thin on the ground as regards a serious type of asymmetric shock – big changes in the balance between savings and investment in any one country, often related to a boom and subsequent bust in the real estate markets. Recent experience highlights the issue. A French real estate bubble formed in the late 1980s and burst just as the tremendous construction and real estate boom developed in post-unification Germany during the first half of the 1990s. As the German bubble subsequently burst even bigger booms developed in Dutch, British, and Spanish residential real estate markets.

The bursting of an asset-market bubble is in general accompanied by a fall in business investment spending and a rise in private savings (household and corporate). The rise in overall savings surplus (or fall in savings deficit) in the economy suffering the bubble collapse in principle goes along with a fall in the equilibrium level of interest rates, a fall in the exchange rate (the national currency becoming cheaper), and a rise in the trade surplus. Growing net exports compensate (in terms of aggregate demand) for a post-bubble fall in domestic demand. In the context of a monetary union it is one interest rate to fit all, and so the post-bubble rise in the savings surplus in one member country (where the bubble had been confined to that country only) would be larger than in the case of monetary independence (where a sharp fall in interest rates would have moderated the rise in savings and fall in investment). That would mean a bigger fall in the domestic price level relative to foreign is required (so as to generate a larger net export surplus).

During the long period of adjustment when the relative fall in the post-bubble economy's price level is taking place, real interest rates would be perversely high there, exacerbating the business cycle downturn. (By contrast, in the floating exchange rate case, a sharp fall in the currency of the post-bubble economy would stir some inflation expectations and help bring down real interest rates even if nominal interest rates are sticky in their decline due to sluggishness of central bank action.) Moreover, the price-level adjustment can be very painful to obtain if indeed the inflation rate in other union countries is low – as then a significant price decline has to take place.

If the asymmetric shock – in this example a real estate market bubble bursting – occurs in the largest economy, in this case Germany, then monetary policy for the union as a whole would adjust in some substantial degree, unlike for the situation of a small economy (which has less significance for the overall macro-economic situation for the entire monetary union which the central bank would be monitoring). In this sense small economies have more danger to fear from asymmetric shock than large – and this runs counter to conventional wisdom that small open economies have least to lose from sacrificing independent monetary policy. (Indeed, the conventional wisdom is wrong on several other scores, described later in this chapter (pp. 19–22) and reviewed further in Chapter 5 (pp. 160–2).) But even in the large economy case, adjustment under the case of monetary union has some evident disadvantages compared to that of the freely floating alternative.

Take the example of German real estate market collapse and slump in the construction industry. The fall of interest rates in the case of monetary union will be more modest than what would occur under an independent Deutschmark (as the European Central Bank focuses on euro-area wide aggregates, not German). More of the adjustment has to take place in the form of the German price level falling relative to that elsewhere in the union and with no help from intra-union exchange rate change. In principle the European Central Bank should take account of the eventual deflationary effect on other union countries (outside Germany) of increasing competition in their traded goods sectors from falling German export prices. It should pre-emptively cut rates by more than would be justified by simply averaging out present inflationary (or deflationary) conditions throughout the euro-area. Indeed, in doing so, it would be imitating what happens in the floating rate case, where a depreciating Deutschmark (triggered by easy German monetary policy) would induce other European central banks also to ease policy so as to offset the drag on their economy from their own currency appreciating against the Deuschmark.

But in practice a supranational central bank in which the senior officials are striving to be good citizens of the union would not be well inclined towards taking a pre-emptive course based on conditions in the largest economy. Such action could lead to charges that the central bank is in effect imperial rather than supranational. The ECB, on performance as revealed so far, has been against giving Germany any special weight above that due arithmetically to its economic size. Instead, some ECB officials even betray satisfaction that the days of European monetary policy being excessively directed by German conditions are now over and rub their hands at the prospect of Germany experiencing the difficulties other countries suffered when they 'had to' adapt to monetary policy as determined by the Bundesbank.

Germany is indeed a special case, as the largest economy in Europe with the biggest potential spill-over impact on to other union countries. As regards medium- and small-size economies there are insights to be gained from the differing experience of the Netherlands and the UK over the past three decades. Both have suffered asymmetric shocks (compared to other European countries) of considerable importance and similarity. First, there have been energy shocks, with both countries being net exporters of energy in comparison with the large net importer status of the EU as a whole. Thus, when energy prices were reaching the sky in the first and second oil shocks (1974 and 1979), the real exchange rate of the guilder and pound came under upward pressure. In the 1980s as energy prices collapsed there was need for real depreciation of both currencies.

In the UK the real depreciation was achieved via a nominal depreciation of sterling. In Holland, there was a long painful process of bringing down Dutch wages relative to German and a sharp rise in unemployment. Also through the 1980s the Netherlands government was involved in the arduous task of curbing public expenditure from the high levels reached in the 1970s (when Finance Minister Wim Duisenberg amongst others had been pump-priming the economy via social welfare spending). That fiscal consolidation – meaning a rise in the national savings surplus – added to the need for real exchange rate depreciation so that external demand could compensate for falling public demand.

A second similar type of shock in both countries (the UK and the Netherlands) have been similar-sized real estate booms and busts. In the early 1980s, both countries were in a bust phase. In the late 1990s and early 2000s both were in a bubble with rapidly rising private consumption, of which the corollary was a falling savings surplus and a rising real exchange rate. In the case of the UK the real appreciation came about via a jump in sterling, whilst in the Netherlands the adjustment came via inflation rising to well above the euro-area average (over 5 per cent p.a. in 2001).

The Dutch central bank under Wim Duisenberg (1982–97) had no sympathy for the view that Holland's asymmetric shocks were best accommodated by a floating, or at least flexibly-adjusted, currency. Indeed, Duisenberg pointed to the mini-devaluation of the guilder against the Deutschmark in the ERM realignment of early 1982 as an illustration of why an independent monetary (and currency) policy was infeasible. In the immediate aftermath of the devaluation there was a spike in long-term Dutch interest rates to a premium over German, apparently reflecting investor unease that the guilder was no longer a quasi-Deutschmark. That rise in long-term rates was more harmful for the Dutch economy, according to the analysis of the central bank under Wim Duisenberg, than any slight stimulus from the currency adjustment.

The Duisenberg case against flexibility is built on a general point. A small open economy might not be able to pursue effectively an independent monetary policy. If the economy is very small and very open (say, like Luxembourg), then residents might simply disregard an independent national money other than as an accounting unit. They would base their investment and borrowing decisions on the most appropriate foreign interest rates and quote prices for goods in the domestic currency simply by translating the foreign currency price into the domestic via the exchange rate. Evidently the Netherlands does not fit into this very small category. Indeed, it is the fifth largest economy in European Monetary Union. But in a small to medium-size economy it might be that inflation and inflation expectations are so sensitive to what happens to the exchange rate that an independent monetary policy based on a domestic anchor – such as an inflation target – is unfeasible. Does the Netherlands fit into that category?

Small can be beautiful for currencies too

The problems of finding a domestic anchor for monetary policy are certainly greater in a small open economy than a large more closed economy. And the anchor found is very unlikely to be as good. Even core inflation (excluding transitory elements such as due to tax, energy, exchange rate, or food-price shocks) might be less than fully reliable. So also might be a monetary aggregate, given that demand for the domestic money in a small open economy could well be less stable than in a large economy due to the likely extent of portfolio shifts in and out of foreign monies.

In the case of the Netherlands in 1982 it is possible in principle that anchor problems lay behind the rise in long-term rates even though the central bank was determined that devaluation should not spill over into a higher core inflation rate. But the fact that the central bank of a small open economy might be unable to find such a good domestic anchor as a large one does not mean that a foreign anchor (for example, the price of foreign currency) is better (in terms of overall economic performance). In practice it could be that the main factor behind the rise of long-term rates in the Netherlands in 1982 in response to the mini-devaluation was a belief in the marketplace that further mini-devaluations were likely to follow, given the obvious need for a cumulative more substantial real devaluation.

If so, the problem with the 1982 devaluation was not the use of currency policy in itself, but the fact that its implementation was far too cautious. The official downward adjustment of the exchange rate was much less than what would have occurred had it been freely floating. As illustration, a 10 per cent fall of the guilder, even if accompanied by some rise in nominal long-term interest rates (on account of the risk that even core inflation might move up transitorily) might have facilitated quicker adjustment of the Netherlands economy to the new reality of lower energy prices, sharp tightening of fiscal policy, and a burst real estate bubble, than the long grind of wages rising by less than in Germany.

A look at the example of Switzerland provides further support for the idea that a small open economy can indeed be an optimum currency area on its own rather than as part of a larger union. Yes, the Swiss National Bank has had no great success in finding a highly reliable domestic anchor – even if its problems in this respect have not been obviously more serious than for many larger central banks. Switzerland, nonetheless, has had considerable success in maintaining an independent money. If Switzerland had been part of the euro-area or, previously, the Deutschmark zone, then interest rates would not have fallen to levels reflecting the huge savings surplus in that country. Instead, interest rates would have been the same as elsewhere in the euro-area or mark zone, the surplus even larger, and the domestic price level would have had to fall relative to that in Germany or the euro-area so as stimulate a much larger trade surplus (net export demand substituting for lower domestic demand).

The Swiss construction sector would have been smaller (in consequence of a higher prevailing level of interest rates), the traded goods and services sector (otherwise described as the export- and import-competing sectors) larger. And the substantial financial business that stems from Switzerland's natural advantage in providing international loan and investment business in its own currency would have been lost. The presumption is that the Netherlands could have been as successful in managing an independent currency as Switzerland, and indeed

Amsterdam might well have flourished to a greater extent as an international financial centre.

The advocate of monetary union might retort to these points in favour of currency independence, even for a small open economy, by suggesting that a small currency is inherently less desirable than a large. In a small open economy an independent money would be less stable in terms of the shopping basket (because of exchange rate fluctuations) and of higher transaction costs (in changing frequently into foreign monies for trade purposes) than a larger one available via currency union. But this point can be overstated. The optimum currency area literature does not allow for the fact that local residents might hold some of their liquid wealth in larger foreign currencies and that information technology allows even small retail outlets to quote dual prices for payment either in the dominant foreign money or the national. Such innovations bring an appreciable reduction in the transaction costs associated with a small national money. In Switzerland, for example, many retail outlets, even in small towns, allow payment to be made in euros or Swiss francs, with the quotation in francs sometimes translated into euros on the basis of a reference franc–euro rate which is near the midpoint of retail bid-offer rates in the foreign currency market.

There is another transactions cost-type argument sometimes used to back the case for monetary union, particularly in Europe. Capital markets require a certain depth to take off which is simply not feasible in small or medium-size independent currencies. The formation of a union allows deep and liquid capital markets to blossom with advantages not just for the European financial industry but also to ultimate borrowers and lenders. And it is indeed true that the Swiss resident, for example, does not have direct access to the same depth of capital markets for borrowing or investing without assuming exchange risk as say his euro-area or US equivalent. On the other hand, the development over recent years of deep and liquid currency and interest rate swap markets does allow indirect access at fractional cost. Swiss investors can buy dollar assets for the purpose of obtaining a particular credit or instrument structure and swap it into Swiss francs so as to eliminate exchange risk. Similarly the Swiss borrower can tap the credit market in whichever currency would obtain the best terms and swap the liability into francs.

Indeed, a hypothetical French or German capital market based on an independently floating French franc and Deutschmark respectively could handle jumbo issues of similar size, albeit of lower frequency, to the present-day euro capital market. Large European and non-European borrowers would make some of the issues now effected in euros in

French francs, and the rest in Deutschmarks. (Investment demand there would not come just from French or German investors, respectively, but also small-country investors, for example, Dutch, buying the paper to swap into their own money.) As a rule they would not turn to the smaller currency capital markets (for example, Dutch guilder) except for perhaps making private placements at low transaction cost to a group of targeted investors. The success of a jumbo issue there would turn on the unlikely situation of a large potential demand from investors having only indirect demand for the paper (swapped back into their preferred currency). In general such indirect investors would find it cheaper to buy packages based on bonds denominated in a medium or large currency (for example, the French franc or guilder), not least because of the greater liquidity of their swap markets. Furthermore, the issuer would have to incur the costs of swapping most of the loan proceeds into his chosen currency.

And there are portfolio diversification benefits for investors that can be derived from the existence of small- and medium-size independent European monies (including the Dutch guilder and French franc). By holding a portfolio of money and bonds in the various denominations they can obtain some insurance against serious monetary errors by any one of the independent European central banks leading to an inflation shock. If there is only one monetary authority in Europe, the ECB, no such diversification is possible. True, a euro-area resident can buy US dollar assets as a hedge against serious policy errors by the ECB. But the US dollar–euro exchange rate is subject to many random influences besides monetary error, whereas intra-European exchange rate fluctuations would tend to be less variable due to the high degree of economic interdependence between the issuing countries.

Indeed, at the level of policy-making the maintenance of a domestic currency provides some protection in the case of small- or medium-sized open economies against the danger of falling into a deflation trap. The government or central bank of a small economy where nominal interest rates are already close to zero and yet not proving low enough to stimulate an upturn in the economy (most probably because the price level is falling so that real interest rates would still be significantly positive) can devalue its currency as the way out. That option is not available for the central bank of a huge monetary area or a large country in that it would be effectively resisted by other large countries or monetary areas. In any case exchange rate depreciation has less of a stimulus effect in a large semi-closed economy than in a small very open economy.

Monetary nihilists at the ECB

Some advocates of monetary union would admit the insurance-type advantage of maintaining currency independence for the small economy, but would decry it as just yet another example of potential beggar-your-neighbour policies which are best suppressed from the viewpoint of global economic welfare. (One small country acting alone might not have significant impact, but what about many small countries acting similarly over a short period of time?) Further, the same advocates sometimes question whether monetary or exchange-rate policy can really be used at all as tools of macro-economic management (other than for potential anti-social behaviour, as described, by the small country). They have no confidence that money has any great influence on the real economy. Much more important are structural policies – improving the performance of the labour market, providing new opportunity for entrepreneurship, and encouraging maximum flexibility at the micro-economic level for prices of individual goods and services to adjust and induce required resource shifts to accommodate any external shocks. As discretionary monetary policies and exchange-rate changes are either ineffective or totally unreliable in their application, it is better to eliminate independent currencies and obtain transaction cost savings thereby and in the new monetary union simply set policy in terms of the very long run, forswearing any tinkering in line with business cycle fluctuations.

These advocates can be described as monetary nihilists, and thus include – as we shall see in the next chapter – leading actors in the euro drama, such as Claude Trichet, Karl Otto Pöhl, Hans Tietmeyer and Wim Duisenberg, amongst others. Edmond Alphandéry, finance minister under French Prime Minister Balladur (1993–5), was a prominent academic exponent – as set out in his book (1998) *La Réforme Obligée: sous le soleil de l'euro*. The monetary nihilists argue, for example, that the preservation of the Deutschmark would not have benefited Germany in the early part of the present decade (2000–10). They rebut all suggestions that the especially deep downturn and hangover of high labour costs in the German economy could have been better dealt with by a sharp devaluation of the Deutschmark (had it still existed) and low interest rates. For them there is no alternative to the painful process of structural change – meaning wage cuts and increased labour flexibility. Germany had no way of returning to economic health other than transforming old-fashioned Rhenish capitalism into a harsher free market order. They would not concede the point that Germany could maintain its social model by devaluing the Deutschmark and driving money interest rates down to zero in line with the low investment opportunity. Then a big export surplus from the enlarged traded goods sector would finance a strong flow of capital exports to countries where the rate of return to capital were substantially higher.

Indeed, the monetary nihilists appear to be making a statement about the type of political economy they favour rather than about the feasibility of any particular social model. Yes, the status quo of the German social economic system might be able to survive in a multi-currency world (meaning intra-European exchange rates again set free), especially where there is sufficient exchange-rate uncertainty to generate risk premiums that isolate domestic interest rates to some extent from the global level. (If there were no risk premiums – meaning higher than otherwise German interest rates – then the price level in Germany would have to be even lower by international comparison so that a bigger export surplus would offset still weaker domestic demand.) But the monetary nihilists want structural change for efficiency's sake.

When it comes to business cycle fluctuations, some of the monetary nihilists would not countenance the proposition that there is substantial benefit from allowing national interest rates to vary unilaterally to reflect lack of synchrony. They argue that in a monetary union where there is just one interest rate a shift in relative price levels can help any one country's economy adjust to cyclical forces that are out of phase with those elsewhere. In practice, however, relative price adjustment is likely to be slow and provide very little relief in the short or medium run. With independent currencies, the interest rate can move down or up relative to those abroad to reflect cyclical differences (the scope to do so being more where exchange risk impedes capital flows), and the exchange rate can vary pro-cyclically (depreciating during a cyclically weak phase and appreciating during a cyclically strong phase – and so bringing about swiftly the relative price changes which are so painfully slow in the absence of independent currencies).

Some monetary nihilists are sympathetic to the view that short-term rates hardly matter at all – rather it is long-term rates that influence decision-making, and these may be more sensitive to fiscal policy than to tinkering with short-term rates. Such a view was expressed strongly by Claude Trichet, for example, in his stubborn defence of the so-called *franc fort* (strong franc) policy (and associated refusal to cut short-term rates boldly as head of the Treasury and subsequently governor of the Banque de France during the French depression of the early 1990s). The best contribution to keeping long-term rates down was pursuing hard-line 'disinflation policies'. And never mind the fact that the currency might be at so high a level as to hurt the export sector seriously. The more it hurts the better – as in the long run this would induce higher productivity there and greater competitiveness. Look at the example of how well Japan did with the super-strong yen and Germany with the strong Deutschmark. These examples have of course subsequently been ridiculed by history. The overvalued yen was a major contributor to Japan's lost decade and the overvalued Deutschmark to Germany's transformation into the sick economy of Europe since the start of the new millennium.

Claude Trichet liked to quote the example of the UK. That country had pulled out of the exchange rate mechanism (of the European Monetary System) in 1992 and slashed short-term interest rates to well below German levels towards exiting from the slump at that time. But long-term rates had not fallen below German levels. That was one reason for France not following the UK example – because in France long-term rates are more important than short in business and household decision-making. On Governor Trichet's criterion, Japanese monetary policy-makers should get top marks, never mind that they allowed their economy to fall into a deflation unprecedented since that in the USA in the 1930s. For by early 2003 long-term interest rates in Japan came close to zero. Trichet and his fellow-travellers in monetary nihilism failed to realize that a highly successful anti-cyclical monetary policy applied against recession – and believed in by market participants – would induce a very positive-sloping yield curve with long-term rates far above short-term. The long-term rates would reflect the bright long-term future when deflation has come to an end and a vibrant recovery would be generating ample investment opportunity.

It is no accident that the monetary nihilists came into such positions of power, both in the steering of the train towards EMU in the 1990s and subsequently in the policy-making council of the European Central Bank. Monetary experts with greater confidence in the power of exchange rates and monetary conditions to influence economic activity over the short and medium term would have been less enthusiastic about the elimination of both tools except at the level of the new union as a whole. Helmut Schlesinger, briefly Bundesbank president in the early 1990s, was one of these experts. The presence and weight of the nihilists on the ECB's policy-making council explains at least in part the reputation of the ECB for inactivity and agnosticism in the power of monetary policy over short or medium periods. They are also a source of the huge emphasis, unusual for a central bank (other than those which are bankrupt of ideas in how to apply monetary policy – such as the Bank of Japan under Governor Hayami), on every policy being tried other than their own – most of all a host of structural change measures and fiscal policy.

The political leaders in France and Germany who drove the process of European monetary union forward towards completion were not economists, and certainly did not realize the dangers that the monetary nihilists could pose to the whole project once completed. It was French President Jacques Chirac who almost precipitated a crisis in German–French relations when he tried in spring 1998 to obtain the appointment of Claude Trichet as ECB president. And Gerhard Schroeder, himself a prominent Social Democrat 'Euro sceptic' in the 1990s, totally failed to realize the importance, once chancellor (from autumn 1998), of appointing a talented and charismatic monetary activist as the new head of the Bundesbank (in place of the retiring Hans Tietmeyer), who would now sit immediately to the right of the president at the ECB policy-making table. It is the role of the political designers of EMU and their relationship to the expert functionaries to which we turn in the next chapter.

2
Founders and Functionaries

In the course of the famous conversations between the author Elie Wiesel and François Mitterrand there is an interchange which throws some light on the force of personal optimism – and belief in progress – that lay behind the process of European monetary union:

Mitterrand: 'One of the greatest incapacities of Man is to imagine the future: he sees it always in the image of the present. ... Take the situation where you have suffered a setback, you feel discredited and sidelined. You have the impression that the situation is irreversible. But in reality life is all powerful and the next morning, the following week, or for those who are patient, one, two years later, the pieces of the puzzle change place. That's my temperament – you would say that I was an optimist. Never have I believed that an obstacle of this order [in talking about his life as a prisoner of war] was insurmountable.'

Wiesel: 'For me, it is the past which I do not succeed in imagining.'

As a thirty-year human endeavour we can certainly say that European monetary integration went through huge swings in its fortune – early promise in the years 1969–71, virtual abandonment in the mid-1970s, incredibly rapid progress during 1988–91, and potentially terminal threats in 1982–3, 1992–3 and 1995–6. As pieces of the puzzle changed from the early 1980s onwards, Mitterrand pressed forward. Yet can we succeed in imagining the total combination of persons and forces that propelled such a project of great social and economic risk (both negative and positive) towards its destination at the cost of considerable human hardship (a prolonged depression in France, Europe's second largest economy)? And by the time of the new union's fifth anniversary it seemed as if the main drivers of the train in the crucial decade from 1988–98 had suffered seriously from the incapacity to imagine the future other than as an image of the present.

The dangers have become only too evident within five years of the euro's launch. The largest economy, Germany, has been in stagnation for three years and denied succour from conventional remedies of aggressive monetary easing and exchange rate depreciation. Could continuing economic decline bring a rebirth of dark nationalistic forces and an eventual rupture of European integration? From the standpoint of 2004 such speculation may still seem way-out. But already political events have been disturbing. In Germany, the Schröder government, weakened by the ailing economy, played the card of anti-Americanism to scrape through to victory in the Bundestag elections of autumn 2002. Early in 2003 Paris, putting to the test its new and long-desired power to direct European foreign policy in the age of the euro, dealt a serious blow to the Atlantic community and awakened fears of Europe reverting to balance of power politics (a France–Germany–Belgium coalition versus a shrunken coalition of European countries still allied to the US).

How did the euro project go forward to completion given these dangers? How aware of what might go wrong were the leading statesmen who drove the process of monetary integration forward? Neither Mitterrand nor Kohl had always been enthusiastic about monetary union. What drove them both passionately to back the project from the middle and end of the 1980s respectively, even though leading monetary economists of the age were at best sceptical and many of their fellow-citizens were deeply hostile? Were the functionaries who made the detailed plans, advised the statesmen, and carried them out themselves blind, cynical, or inappropriately zealous?

How sincere was Mitterrand's enthusiasm for monetary union?

François Mitterrand and Helmut Kohl holding hands in a war cemetery at Verdun in autumn 1984, to mark the sixty-eighth anniversary of the terrible battle which raged there during the First World War, is perhaps the driving image of the great last lap of the historical process which brought the euro into existence. Both men, though they had complex and differing agendas behind their decision to apply the accelerator to the monetary integration train in late spring 1988, were driven overall by the desire for lasting peace in Europe and the conviction that a final and irreversible reconciliation between France and Germany was essential for that purpose. Both believed that together they represented the last chance for monetary union to take place, and that this would ensure everlasting peace between their two countries. After them would come a generation of leaders with no first-hand knowledge of war between France and Germany. Mitterrand had experienced personally the military defeat of spring 1940, subsequent imprisonment in Germany, Vichy collaboration, and Resistance. Kohl had grown up with the horrors of Verdun related to him by his father, who had fought there, and he himself as a teenager had witnessed the devastation of wartime bombing on his hometown Ludwigshafen.

The quest for reconciliation was nothing new in French–German relations. Konrad Adenauer and Charles de Gaulle had set the stage in the early 1960s. Indeed, de Gaulle had a good knowledge of German language, literature, and philosophy, which he cultivated well into his old age (see Barnavi, 1985). But his viewpoint had remained essentially nationalist. Paul-Henri Spaak (one of the great post-war fathers of European integration) wrote: 'De Gaulle claims that he supports a united Europe, but he only conceives this as under French hegemony.'

Mitterrand himself was immersed in some aspects of German culture and history. He was fascinated by Prussian history (in particular the cultural aspects), was a fan of Heinrich Böll, and 'liked the prosaic Germany of the potato' (see Sauzay, 1999). He was sensitive to the great suffering of the German people, even during the Third Reich and immediately following its destruction. 'He neither supported aversion to nor distrust of Germany. Nor did he fall into wonderment as some parts of the French press. His wholly relaxed, fully impartial view, and feeling, allowed him to avoid inferiority or superiority complexes in dealing with Germany' (Sauzay, 1999). Unusually for a French statesman, his memoirs were published under the title *De L'Allemagne, de la France* (Of Germany, Of France). Lacouture, his famous biographer, describes Mitterrand as a Germanophile French head of state (see Lacouture, 1999).

Some critics have questioned the profoundness of Mitterrand's commitment to European integration. The zig-zag of his career through such grey areas as student affiliation to a far-right group in Paris of the mid-1930s, dual membership of the wartime resistance and (low-ranking) role in the Vichy government, friendship and suspected sheltering from prosecution of Bousquet (ex-Vichy police chief responsible for the deportation of Jews), wreaths at the grave of Pétain, an arranged assassination attempt on his own life (during the Fourth Republic), turning a blind eye as minister of justice in the 1950s to use of torture by French intelligence forces in Algeria, and late embracing of socialism (and forming an alliance with the communists) only to do a U-turn within two years of taking power – all of this suggests that everything may not be as it seems. Was the adoption of Europe as the central theme of his presidency in the first half of 1984, after the failure of his socialist agenda, any more than an opportunistic step based on survival strategy and electoral arithmetic?

Laurent Fabius in his book *Les Blessures de la vérité* (Wounds of Truth) (1995) answers the question directly and artistically in describing Mitterrand's character as having a property of

> fundamental metaphysical ambivalence, which makes him see everything as it is and as its opposite. Europe is one of the strongest convictions of his life, but nothing is worth a piece of French land. France is his passion, part of himself. But he places above all that the European dream. Mitterrand seduces by the duality of his action and of his relationship to the world. This ambivalence, which he does not make explicit, the French people have understood. Indeed it corresponds to their state of mind in a certain fashion. It translates and permits the passage from one period of history to another, from one geography (hexagonal France) to another (France in Europe), from one century to another. Mitterrand is the double face of France ... Ambivalence lies behind his saying that it is necessary to give time to Time. Only time can transform beings and things to the point at which they present their other face, their other possibility – in brief that they become what they are.

Ambivalence is also evident in Mitterrand's attitude to war and peace. At the age of seventeen he had won a prize in a national essay competition (sponsored by a Catholic institute concerned amongst other things with the rights of Catholic veterans from the First World War), and his writing had included a passage where dead soldiers lament from their graves about the lack of understanding for their sacrifice. He writes an article in a journal following the Anschluss (1938):

> it is perhaps true that it would be mad for France to go to war to save a lost peace (of the Versailles Treaty); the life of one man is without doubt more serious than the destruction of a state ... Nonetheless, I experience some anxiety. Among the enthusiastic crowd of Inn and Vienna (who are welcoming the Nazi troops) I detect the agony of one face leaning over the Blue Danube and I try in vain to see more amongst the tumult of the river. Before the triumphal march of the God of Bayreuth in the land of Mozart I know that a great sacrilege is about to occur. I experience a sort of shame, as if I shared responsibility.

The journalist Pierre Péan, in his book (*Une Jeunesse française*) (1994) about Mitterrand's early life, comments on this passage that it reveals a very 'realpolitik' approach to the situation, a deep sense of history – with some moral concern only appearing at the end. That is a harsh, albeit not obviously faulty, judgement. And there can be no doubting of Mitterrand's realpolitik approach to European integration, even though his grand aim was not devoid of idealism. At a crucial point in the nuclear arms race of the early 1980s he declared in a speech to the Bundestag (1983) his support for NATO's 'two-track strategy' (new deployment in Germany of US medium-range missiles in response to Russian nuclear build-up in Eastern Europe). Thus he abandoned in part French unilateralism in nuclear defence policy so as to help the new chancellor, Helmut Kohl, on the eve of his first electoral test in a climate where there was a strong current of anti-Americanism and pacifism.

Later, seizing the opportunity of the French presidency of the EU in the first half of 1984, Mitterrand moved the agenda forward and ended the stand-off with the UK about budgetary contributions. He gained the consent of Helmut Kohl to the appointment of a Frenchman as EC Commission president from January 1985 with the proviso that this should be none other than Jacques Delors. Immediately after his re-election as president in spring 1988 Mitterrand concluded a deal with Chancellor Kohl to set up a committee to draft plans for monetary union, taking advantage of Germany's concern to show good faith in its commitment to Western European integration at a time when Bonn was making new overtures to the East (encouraged by a thawing of relations with the Soviet Union under President Gorbachev). And at the historic moment of the Berlin Wall opening, when France again occupied the six-month rotating presidency of the EU, Mitterrand went about obtaining Kohl's agreement to setting up an intergovernmental conference that would push forward with monetary union. Finally, at the crucial EU Summit in Maastricht (December 1991), Mitterrand succeeded in getting a fixed date by which monetary union should take place entered into the treaty.

Some historians argue that none of this could have happened without the additional factor of Kohl and Mitterrand relating to each other so well. Giscard d'Estaing (who Mitterrand defeated to become president in May 1981) would have had, at best, a frosty relationship with Kohl, whilst Kohl's predecessor as chancellor, Helmut Schmidt, who got on well with Giscard d'Estaing, by most accounts would not have hit it off with Mitterrand (indeed, there was an overlap from spring 1981 until autumn 1982 during which relations were cordial but Schmidt, as a trained economist, was deeply suspicious of Mitterrand's brand of socialism and his new economic policy). There have been many published anecdotes of the warmness in the relationship between the two heads of states – Mitterrand's telephone call to Kohl about his son following a serious car accident, Mitterrand's recounting to Kohl of how when being taken back to his prisoner of war camp an elderly German woman had risked severe punishment in offering him food (and saying to him not to believe that all Germans are bad), Kohl's efforts, when very ill towards the end of his presidency, to spare Mitterrand embarrassment.

One much commented-upon dimension of the personal relationship was its extension to direct financial aid – the allegation that Mitterrand arranged for cash to go directly into the coffers of Kohl's political party in early 1994. The commissions were allegedly paid by French agents in the form of 'suitcase cash' as part of the notorious 'Leuna affair'. The French state-run Elf Acquitaine was acquiring the Leuna complex in East Germany under a procedure in which state enterprises there were being repackaged where possible for disposal to the private sector – including foreign bidders. It is not plausible that the head of Elf, appointed by Mitterrand, would have authorized secret payments simply to secure the Leuna complex for his enterprise. Much more likely is that the commissions were related to a crucial Bundestag election looming later that year. The cash inflow critically strengthened the position of Kohl against any possible rivals who might have been less motivated in the direction of seeing that the EMU train reached its destination. No serious observer has ever suggested that Mitterrand bought Kohl's assent to EMU or, more colourfully, to selling the Bundesbank. Rather, the issue is that Mitterrand helped his friend Kohl at a key point to sustain his position of power to reach the aim of monetary union that they were both now pursuing with equal ardour.

Ardour did not stem from economic conviction at all. Indeed, Mitterrand could be dismissive of the economic arguments. At the decisive moment in early 1983, when his economic councillors were divided on the merit of the franc staying in the fixed exchange rate mechanism (ERM) of the European Monetary System (EMS), Mitterrand decided on the basis of political ideal and ambition in favour of continued membership. Claude Cheysson, his foreign minister at the time, later wrote that 'the decision in favour of Europe was deeply ingrained in the president. European solidarity – that means German in effect – was an absolute priority.' Europe, for Mitterrand, did not include the UK. Even so, his version of 'Continentalism' stopped short of the distinct anti-'Anglo-Saxon' sentiment found amongst several other leading French actors in the EMU drama (including, in particular, Raymond Barre). In the French referendum debate of 1972 called by President Pompidou to approve the UK's entry into the EC, Mitterrand had campaigned on the No side. Some snippets of evidence on Mitterrand's 'Continental policy', come from Aeschmann and Riché's revealing book *La Guerre de Sept Ans: Histoire secrète du franc fort, 1989–96* (The Seven Years War: secret history of the strong franc policy, 1989–96).

For example, in January 1991, on the eve of the crucial negotiations leading up to the Maastricht Treaty, the finance minister, Pierre Bérégovoy, pleaded the case for proceeding with the development of a common European money alongside existing national ones rather than merging them all into one any time soon. Bérégovoy, himself an Anglophile (an attitude that went back to his years in the Resistance, and expressed in the comment he would make in private, 'It is they who won the war and liberated us, we should not forget that'), could not imagine Europe without the UK as a full member. The president replied to him that the Germans were opposed to the concept of a common currency in competition to the Deutschmark. 'I [Mitterrand] myself was opposed for a long time to the concept of a European central bank. But France will have more influence on a European central bank than it does today on the mark. ... This is no time for a reversal of alliances. Our ally is Germany. The British are allies of the US.' This exchange is not evidence of anti-Americanism, or anti-English sentiment, but a realpolitik view that 'one will never make Europe if we wait for the British'. And when it came to the German–French relationship, the president commented previously, 'It is necessary to create this axis, but above all it must not be made obvious.'

Mitterrand's view that France would have a bigger say in monetary policy run for Europe by a European central bank than by the Bundesbank was the kernel of his economic case. This begs the issue as to why those were the only options being considered by French policy-makers – a monetary satellite to Germany or a member of a European monetary union. Why could there not be an independent French monetary policy? And when it came to the influence that France might have as a member of monetary union, Mitterrand and his advisers were surely overcalculating. Even if the first or second president of the European Central Bank were French, how much power would he or she have sitting in an independent policy-making council of nearly twenty members? Much would depend on the talent and the charisma of the individual chosen. Even then, would that French individual use his influence in the narrow interests of France or would his first allegiance be to the welfare of the euro-area as a whole?

The apologist for Mitterrand can argue that he did not fully realize how independent of political influence the European Central Bank was to be – even though this was well spelt out in the Maastricht Treaty (December 1991). During the French referendum campaign (autumn 1992), Mitterrand had said categorically on TV that governments would have the final say on monetary policy, not the central bankers: 'The central bank will take no decisions! It is the European Council which will decide! ... The technicians of the European Central Bank are obliged in the monetary field to carry out the decisions of the Council [of ministers] – that means, by the politicians elected by the people!' At best that was wishful thinking about how far French diplomacy might resuscitate (in the years between the signing of the Treaty and the start of the monetary union) the concept of a European Economic Council as an effective counterweight to the ECB, even though it had been abandoned under German pressure during the negotiations leading up to Maastricht.

How did Kohl steer Germany into two flawed monetary unions?

If there was wishful thinking at the opposite end of the French–German policy-making axis it concerned the long-term strength of the German economy. Chancellor Kohl and Bundesbanker Hans Tietmeyer overestimated the competitive ability of Germany to withstand two fundamental monetary changes within less than a decade. First there had been the hugely expensive and severely criticized (including by the Bundesbank) monetary union between the two Germanys in 1990. Then, later in the same decade (1990s), Germany became locked in European monetary union at an exchange rate making much of its industry unprofitable now that domestic demand had cooled from boom-time levels. Both unions might have worked well for Germany if wages could have fallen sharply in the East and to a smaller extent in the West. But rigid German labour markets were unsuited to such an adjustment. Implicitly Helmut Kohl believed in a new economic miracle for his country, more than thirty years after the end of the Great Miracle (1948–64).

Anyhow, for Kohl monetary union was primarily a means to a political end. The offer of monetary union to East Germany in early 1990 had been made as a catalyst to political union (between the Federal Republic and the DDR). Kohl also realized that the prompt offer would bolster the popularity of his party (CDU) on the eve of the first free parliamentary elections in the East. His consent to monetary union of Germany with France and other European countries was made as part of a political strategy aimed at securing German reunification within an integrated Europe. Moreover, key industrial lobbies in Germany – the banks and large exporting companies – were calling for European Monetary Union (see Meier, 1997).

The overwhelming support of the German banks and big business for EMU was puzzling even without the benefit of hindsight. Surely the banks would lose from a regime change in which the new European money was to replace the Deutschmark as the number two currency in the world? German banks had a competitive advantage versus say Dutch or French banks in Deutschmark markets but not obviously in euro markets. There would now be a level playing field. The overriding view of leading German bankers was that in a bigger playing field (euro markets would be larger than the old Deutschmark ones) their institutions would be able to capture more business, even though their home currency advantage had gone. As regards big business, their leaders appeared to have no foreboding that locking Germany into monetary union without a large fall of the Deutschmark prior to union would put them at a long-term competitive disadvantage. Their immediate and overriding fear was that the breakdown of the train to monetary union could spark a new big rise of the Deutschmark that would make their competitive disadvantage even larger. It was just not part of their mindset that without monetary union the next big move of the Deutschmark might well be downwards.

And so Helmut Kohl did not have to fear a backlash amongst his party backers from pushing forward with monetary union. Indeed, the cause of EMU had boosted Kohl's notorious slush fund (revealed in the aftermath of his autumn 1998 election defeat). Most important were the commissions received from Paris in the 'Leuna affair'. Also cash streamed in from anonymous private individuals or organizations and powerful German companies. The fund was crucial to Helmut Kohl's power base because much of the money was funnelled to the regional CDU parties. These payments explain how Kohl imposed the discipline that made the CDU a formidable election-fighting machine.

There is no basis for speculating that slush fund operations tilted Helmut Kohl in favour of EMU. The issue is whether Kohl betrayed the cause of German democracy. Opponents to EMU – of which there were many in his own party, its Bavarian sister (CSU) and the opposition

SPD – were sidelined from power at least in part by Kohl's access to illegal funds. Within the CDU, rivals were politically extinguished or exiled to provincial posts. Kohl insisted on complete party loyalty and discipline. Even when backbenchers travelled abroad, Kohl personally authorized the trip and knew precisely where they were going and with whom they were meeting. He controlled his party with an iron grip. The slush fund casts a shadow over the democratic validity of Germany's passage to monetary union but not on the sincerity of Helmut Kohl's European beliefs.

Like his 'spiritual father', Konrad Adenauer, Kohl believed that French–German friendship was the key to constructing Europe. And he considered Mitterrand as a loyal and dependable partner, just as de Gaulle had been to Adenauer. Yes, there was now reconciliation. But Kohl recalled (from the history books) the false hopes at the signing of the Locarno Treaty in 1925, when many contemporaries saw the Briand–Stresseman partnership as heralding a new age of peace. Eight years later Hitler was chancellor of Germany. A binding of Germany and France together in the framework of European integration was the best guarantee of peace – and from 1988 onwards Kohl became growingly convinced that monetary union would be remarkably strong glue. During his last eight years as chancellor (1990–8), Helmut Kohl pursued monetary union with a determination based on the sincere belief that this really would banish the spectre of war from Europe. Later he confided to a TV interviewer that he would have retired in 1996 had he not feared that the EMU train would become derailed if he left the driving seat.

Adenauer had once counselled Kohl that in dealing with France he should always bow once to the German flag and twice to the French. In reality that did not mean that Kohl would discourage his senior officials and the Bundesbank from pushing their French opposite numbers for the hardest deal possible – as the final shape of monetary union was to illustrate (much closer to the German than French blueprint). Yet there was no doubting the sincerity of Kohl's idealism about Europe. He was not one of those statesmen whom Bismarck described as 'Europe being in their mouths for the purpose of gaining from other powers something they did not dare to demand in their own name', even though Kohl's European record was not without blemish.

There had been the unilateral bid (without consulting European partners) for a German confederation within weeks of the Berlin Wall opening, and the drawn-out renunciation of all claims by a united Germany to lands East of the Oder-Neisse line. (Nor were the attempts of the chancellor's office to explain the delay in terms of pre-empting any jump in support for the far right at the forthcoming elections in East Germany wholly satisfactory.) In the charged days of late 1988, however, when the East German communist regime was crumbling, Mitterrand had also made some blunders in terms of Franco-German and West European solidarity. His visit to President Gorbachev to discuss the German situation and his meetings in East Germany with the reformist communist leaders are still debated by political analysts as to their real significance. Blemishes aside, Kohl remained true to the principle that German unification and European integration (including Germany) were opposite sides of the same coin.

History – the tide of events – and skilful persuasion (particularly by Jacques Delors) rather than self-inspiration turned Kohl into a champion for monetary union. In his first few years as chancellor (from autumn 1982) the main foreign policy preoccupation was responding to the new Soviet nuclear threat. At that time, French–German co-operation had taken the form of Paris backing fully Kohl's support for US nuclear rearmament on German soil against a wave of anti-US and pacifist populism (in Germany). In a second stage (1984–7), Kohl had embraced Mitterrand's drive to reinvigorate the 'European process', involving in particular the Single Europe Act (EU Treaty establishing the framework for the Single Market). The efforts of Jacques Delors to tie the Single Europe Act to a new push towards monetary union had not been fully endorsed by Bonn. Indeed Germany had obtained agreement that any progress towards monetary union would require first a revision of the Rome Treaty. (The future Bundesbank president, Hans Tietmeyer, then Kohl's top economic diplomat at G7 and EC meetings, had drafted the text.) Doubtless Kohl, in his initial coolness to European Monetary Union, was influenced by the scepticism of the Bundesbank and the potential domestic unpopularity of sacrificing the Deutschmark.

In Germany it was Foreign Minister Genscher who (as early as in 1987) was first to promote the aim of European Monetary Union, realizing that the new opportunities in Ostpolitik opening up as Gorbachev pursued his reform course in the Soviet Union must be balanced by Germany demonstrating further its commitment to West European integration. The success of Genscher's small FDP party in the 1987 Bundestag elections had strengthened his position in the coalition cabinet. The re-election of Mitterrand as president of France in spring 1988 (and the return of his Socialist party to power after two years of cohabitation with the centre-right parties) set the historic background to the Franco-German Summit in Évian (2 June 1988). On a terrace with a panoramic view over Lake Geneva, President Mitterrand, flanked by his key European policy advisers Jacques Attali and Elisabeth Guigou, committed his government towards abolishing all controls on international capital flows (and in particular capital exports from France).

Abolition (of exchange restrictions) was a key component of the 'Europe without frontiers' (albeit not part of the Single Market Act, but implemented by an accompanying directive) being promoted by Jacques Delors in Brussels. It was also a repeated demand of Bundesbank President Pöhl (who saw the continued exchange restrictions in France and Italy as inconsistent with European monetary integration). In exchange, Chancellor Kohl undertook to use the opportunity of Germany's current presidency of the EC to support the setting up of a committee to consider European Monetary Union (the proposal was adopted at the EC summit in Hanover a few weeks later). Support for a committee (headed by the EC Commission president) and its subsequent findings did not yet signify enthusiasm (on the part of Chancellor Kohl) for monetary union in the short or the medium term. As one member of the Delors Committee, Eric Hoffmeyer, president of the Danish central bank subsequently wrote, neither he nor any of his fellow committee-members thought that union would come in their lifetime. It was German unification that ultimately swung Kohl behind key initiatives in 1990–1 that would shorten dramatically the prospective journey to EMU.

What made Jacques Delors run?

The speed of the eventual timetable took even Jacques Delors, president of the EU Commission (1985–95), by surprise. He had imagined back in 1989 when his report on monetary union was published that an intergovernmental conference would not be called before 1993, once the Single Market programme was complete (target date 1992 for Europe without frontiers). And surely more than a decade would elapse from the conference to monetary union being complete! But Jacques Delors, no more than anyone else, could forecast German unification and the profound impact that would have on the journey to European Monetary Union. Even so, when Delors had taken over as president of the European Commission in January 1985 he already had a clear vision of how to relaunch Europe.

A first priority was to push forward with the Single Market programme, for which there was general support. Second, building on the success of the Single Market, there should be a new initiative towards monetary union – a much more controversial and less widely supported step. The link would be the freeing of capital movements (essential to the Single Market) and the growing integration of goods and services markets. His strategy was to sell monetary union as essential to completing the Single Market – by removing barriers in the form of exchange risk and wild currency fluctuations, more menacing now in that capital was free to move.

What drove Delors to push forward with monetary union? At one level there was the old idea going back to the founding fathers of the Common Market (for example, Jean Monnet) that Europe would be built through growing technical co-operation – and political integration would follow. Monetary union would prove to be the catalyst to growing political integration. Delors had come round to the view that socialism could not be practised in one country on its own. That view was based on (not proved by!) the failed socialist experiment in France during 1981–3, of which he had had first-hand experience as finance minister (remaining in that post until mid-1984). Delors believed that a soft type of socialism – on the German model of Rhenish capitalism – could be built at the Europe-wide level. Creating Europe was not a goal in itself but for 'developing a project of civilization...The mission of Europe will never be to govern the world or to impose by force its own idea of well-being. It consists, rather, of resuscitating and projecting Europe's best spiritual traditions.'

One biographer, Milesi (1997), described Delors as being fascinated by the German model. He would quote the German emphasis on investment. 'Profits are conditions of investment which are the jobs of tomorrow.' (All such comments look anachronistic in view of the ailing German economy of the early 2000s.) He extolled German anti-monopoly policy (the functioning of its cartel office). When, as finance minister, he played a lead-role in the U-turn out of unilateral socialism to becoming a well-behaved German monetary satellite, he was acting consistently with his perception of Germany as the example to follow.

Back in the 1950s, when Delors was climbing the ladder at the Banque de France (where his father, after being severely handicapped in the First World War, had worked all his life as a messenger) and active simultaneously in the Christian trade union movement, he had opposed France's entry into the Common Market. He feared that France would be swamped by the stronger German economy. Two articles which he authored in *La Jeune République* warned that France would become the German dupe. The Common Market was a scheme for imposing liberal economics on France and losing its sovereignty to make an alternative choice. Since then he had become more optimistic about the ability of the French economy to adapt to the German model and more pessimistic about there being any alternative course. Into the 1960s and 1970s, Delors shifted to a realization that profits play a key role in generating investment and growth, but he remained suspicious of markets. As finance minister he often repeated the phrase that 'markets are myopic' – a belief that was consistent with his participation in the economic planning process which successive French governments promoted through the 1950s and 1960s and also, incidentally, was shared by Raymond Barre (whose role in European monetary integration, first at the EC Commission then later as French prime minister, is discussed in Chapter 4).

As a socialist and trade unionist, experienced in the economic planning process, and pro-profits and investment, Jacques Delors came to the attention of de Gaulle's prime minister, Pompidou, in the late 1960s and then to President Pompidou's first prime minister, Chaban-Delmas (a loyalist of de Gaulle from the days of the Resistance, but a centrist politically). Both Pompidou and Chaban-Delmas were intent on shifting economic and social policy towards capturing the middle ground in French politics, and were influenced by the turmoil following the 1968 student riots and general strike. Delors accepted the invitation of joining the cabinet of Chaban-Delmas as a counsellor. Mitterrand never overlooked this membership of a Gaullist-led government and an earlier refusal to join his presidential campaign team in 1965, even though Delors was to navigate with consummate skill through the subsequent struggles inside the Socialist party. Delors would not ally himself with Michel Rocard in his centrist challenge to Mitterrand at the Metz party conference (1979) – perceiving correctly that he had a greater future as a centrist under Mitterrand than with Rocard. In the same year as the Metz conference Delors became a Socialist member of the European Parliament in the first direct elections to that body, where he gained the chairmanship of the Monetary Affairs Committee (just at the start of the European Monetary System).

Delors recognized early on that the young Laurent Fabius was a serious future challenger to his prospect of becoming prime minister, or even remaining as finance minister, under a Mitterrand administration. Fabius, unlike Delors, was in the inner circle of Mitterrand – and, indeed, in summer 1984 Mitterrand promoted Fabius directly into the premiership, having just, at the instigation of Kohl, nominated Delors as the next head of the EU Commission. (Famously, Kohl had said that he would accept a Frenchman, but only one with the initials JD. Mitterrand had first sounded out the German view on his foreign minister, Cheysson, but Kohl regarded him as too close to his own foreign minister, Genscher. Delors had impressed Kohl in the course of intensive negotiations between France and Germany during the French presidency of the EU in the first half of 1984.)

In the Mitterrand–Delors–Kohl triangle, relations were at their best (in terms of mutual esteem) between Mitterrand and Kohl and between Delors and Kohl. The Mitterrand–Delors relationship was vital but not warm. Delors, a committed Catholic, made a point about the strong Catholic background of Mitterrand. In his eyes, Mitterrand was a Christian who had taken a wrong turning (towards total secularism), but nonetheless was Catholic at base. But for Mitterrand, Delors was 'one of the Christians of the second left, of this tormented and mischievous race which will never produce a great politician [*homme politique*]' (Meyret, 1994). Mitterrand realized that Delors was the best of his team on TV and he confided to one biographer that he had appointed him as finance minister so as to 'reassure the French'.

By contrast, Delors' relations to Kohl deepened in his new role as president of the European Commission. Delors had brushed up his German on becoming president (albeit that Delors and Kohl spoke together in English). In Bonn Delors was viewed as a Frenchman who understood the Germans and respected their culture and traditions. Biographers have commented that both Kohl and Delors were united in a certain simplicity – and there was the link of the first as a Christian Democrat on the left and the second as a Christian Socialist on the right. On the opening day of the trial in 1986 of Barbie (the Gestapo butcher of Lyons), Delors told a German newspaper that German youth should still be proud of their fatherland. Delors and Kohl would dine together in Bonn, Brussels, Paris, or half-way. Delors was quite ready to enjoy salacious jokes with the chancellor. Delors was ahead of the French government in accepting German unification once the Berlin Wall opened and quickly in spring 1990 prepared the text that would allow East Germany immediate integration into the European Community. Already in December 1989 Delors endorsed clearly the expansion of the European Community to Eastern Europe – an objective of Bonn. Delors was the guest of honour at the reunification ceremonies in Germany on 3 October 1990.

The relationship between Kohl and Delors was crucial in the first half of 1988, when Germany held the presidency of the EU and the way was being laid for the Hannover Summit (in June) to endorse the setting up of a committee under Delors to design a framework for European Monetary Union. In a conversation with the journalist Dominique

Wolton, Delors later claimed that initially in early 1988 monetary union was not high up his agenda. The priority was pushing forward with the Single Market programme. But he soon found French Prime Minister Balladur and German Foreign Minister Genscher knocking on his door. (Balladur was not banging for monetary union in terms close to anything that subsequently emerged, but rather the creation of a European central bank which would deepen the European monetary system and issue a new European currency.) That had been the catalyst to opening direct conversations with Chancellor Kohl about the topic. The Hannover Summit (June 1988) endorsed the setting up of a committee under Delors but, on the insistence of Kohl and Mitterrand, one that was mainly made up of central bankers. Mitterrand had opposed the inclusion of finance ministers on the principle that if you want to conclude an agricultural treaty you do not invite agriculture ministers and in practice because of doubts about the enthusiasm of his finance minister, Pierre Bérégovoy, for European monetary union.

What drove Delors – other than personal ambition – to seize the moment (spring 1988) for driving forward the European monetary project? Advancement of French interest (as he and the Mitterrand

2   **The euro means the end of nationalisms**
Source: Chappatte, *Die Weltwoche*, January 1999.

administration saw it) cannot be ignored as a factor. In the 1992 referendum campaign Delors told his fellow citizens that 'if we do not make Europe now it will mean the marginalization of France'. On another occasion he said that 'creating Europe is a way of regaining that room for manoeuvre necessary for a certain idea of France'. And fleetingly, during the crisis meeting of EU finance ministers in summer 1993 (31 July–1 August), Delors embraced a French proposal that the Deutschmark should temporarily exit the European exchange rate mechanism and the remaining currencies anchor themselves to the French franc (see Chapter 4).

There was also an element of anti-Americanism that even blended well with the policy positions of his Gaullist predecessors and followers. During his three years as finance minister, Delors did not cease denouncing the 'egoism of the US' – and stigmatized Washington for building its prosperity at the expense of the rest of the world (Meyret, 1994). In *L'Unit d'un homme* (Unity of a man) (a series of conversations between Delors and Wolton), Delors asks his interviewer

> to remember the justified struggle of General de Gaulle against the imperialism of the dollar … The creation of a European money will permit Europe to oblige the Americans to respect themselves a certain number of rules of the game. The realization of monetary union will be an important step towards establishing a more effective international monetary system. We (the Europeans) will be better armed to deal with disturbances created by the great American bubble … A European money will be an instrument of power.

This train of analysis was deeply flawed. When the great US bubble did burst, it was the newly formed euro-area that suffered the most.

Of course, some of the anti-American comments could be regarded as little more than opportunistic – in particular those made around the time of the U-turn in policy by the Mitterrand administration away from socialism and towards Europe. It was easier to blame Messrs Reagan and Volcker than flaws in the government's own programme. But the few quotes above do suggest a more enduring soft European nationalism, which sometimes went along with resentment at perceived abuses of US economic power. A more difficult issue is whether Catholicism was an influence on the nature of Delors' commitment to the cause of European monetary union.

Aeschmann and Riché (1999) in recounting the history of the 'Seven Years War' (1989–96) over the *franc fort* note the extent to which

3   The future of Chirac and Kohl spins on the euro
Source: Hachfeld, *Neues Deutschland*, April 1996.

Christian metaphors were used by proponents to justify the short-term hardships. 'At the top of the Treasury and the Monetary Committee of the Banque de France (founded in 1994) were several practising Catholics. The repeated calls to sacrifice (for the future benefits) could be read as the reminiscences of a certain Christian concept of the redemption.' And many years later (*Le Monde*, 31 January, 2001) in a newspaper dialogue with the Czech president Vaclav Havel on the topic of 'La Grande Europe', Delors repeated his regret that the European Charter of Human Rights did not mention Europe's Christian heritage. But Delors also stressed that Europe is beyond simplistic definitions, whether Social Democrat or Christian. And at no time did the German chancellor, French president or prime minister, show disregard for the key importance of the short-term electoral timetable – never mind what European redemption might lie further ahead, according to their more devout advisers.

Nonetheless there were some electoral miscalculations by the French and German leaders who drove the EMU project forward – the greatest perhaps by Jacques Chirac, president of France from May 1995. His decision in autumn 1995 to push ahead with severe fiscal tightening in the midst of an economic downturn so as to ensure that France would come within grasp of attaining the budget limits stipulated in the Maastricht

Treaty may well have averted a serious derailment of the EMU train. (That proposition is not self-evident, as we shall see in Chapter 4, where a hypothetical alternative high-risk strategy of brinkmanship towards Germany and the Banque de France by the new Chirac administration is reviewed.) But Chirac, unduly influenced (according to the Paris rumour-mill) by his chief of staff at the Élysée, Dominique de Villepin (see more below), seriously underestimated the electoral fall-out – the spring 1997 legislative elections bringing one of the biggest shocks of French political history, with the overturning of the huge parliamentary majority for the centre-right parties.

Jacques Chirac takes France on the final journey to the promised land of EMU

The previous history of Chirac did not obviously suggest any great attachment to Europe, European Monetary Union, or any other ideal. Chirac had gone into electoral battle with his neo-Gaullist forces (the RPR) in the European Parliament elections of 1979 on a nationalist anti-Europe ticket, and had suffered badly. Then came the change. His old anti-European advisers were out. In came Jérôme Menod, the scion of a patrician protestant family, and Édouard Balladur, an ex-counsellor of President Pompidou. Chirac's government of 1986–8 (with himself as prime minister in 'co-habitation' with Mitterrand as president) had signed the Single European Act (1987) and its finance minister Balladur had opened a diplomatic initiative in early 1988 in favour of setting up a European central bank. Some commentators have suggested that the pro-Europe leaning of Chirac's government in the mid-1980s turned on intelligence that Soviet Union President Gorbachev was making overtures to Chancellor Kohl (Germany loosening its commitment to West European integration in exchange for re-unification?).

Chirac, as prime minister at that time (1986–8), had already established a close relationship with Chancellor Kohl, visiting him at his home in Ludwigsburg. Like de Gaulle, Chirac was always a supporter of the German nation. In visiting the Berlin Wall in 1983 (as mayor of Paris and Gaullist party boss) he had given a speech that the two parts of Germany should form one nation. 'It is humanly and naturally necessary that they regain unity.' In 1987 Chirac had agreed that France would reduce its nuclear arsenal as part of a 'null solution' with the Soviet Union regarding the withdrawal of nuclear missiles from Eastern Europe. Chirac's vision was of Europe as a Great Power on the international stage with French diplomacy at its helm, but with as little sacrifice of national sovereignty as possible. The aim was 'a Europe for France, at the command of France, and not Europe for Europe. Europe is inevitably under construction – better to accompany the movement rather than fight against windmills' (Madelin, 1998)

With a socialist government again in power from 1988 to 1993, Chirac had albeit with some delay taken a stand in favour of the Maastricht Treaty in the autumn 1992 referendum. Cynical commentators maintained that the decision to back Maastricht was essentially driven by political calculation rather than conviction. If Chirac had sided with the opposition to Maastricht (around 50 per cent of his own party was against) he risked eclipse. In the looming spring 1993 parliamentary elections the Socialists were expected to suffer a landslide defeat. But if Mitterrand had meanwhile won the referendum then he would appoint as next prime minister the pro-Maastricht Giscard d'Estaing from the centre-right UDF party rather than an anti-Maastricht member of Chirac's neo-Gaullist party. (Of course, if Chirac had opposed Maastricht and swung the Gaullist vote behind him, the referendum result might have indeed been against the proposed treaty rather than narrowly in favour. Then Mitterrand could not have sidelined Chirac.) But other commentators suggest that Chirac was already convinced of the Treaty's virtue and the delay in backing it was due mainly to managing internal Gaullist party conflict over the issue.

By 1992 Chirac was already taking considerable notice of advice from Alain Juppé, a brilliant young man whom the Gaullist leader found in

4 Chirac and Kohl cradle their euro baby
Source: Hachfeld, *Le Monde*, December 1996.

some measure the mirror-image of himself. He had been budget minister under Chirac's government of 1986–8 and then became general secretary of the Gaullist party. (In that last role public prosecutors were much later to charge Juppé with authorizing the practice of putting party workers on the payroll of Paris City Hall or of private companies 'successful' in winning contracts from Paris City Hall. There Chirac reigned as Mayor and Juppé functioned as Treasurer.) In the Balladur government (1993–5) Juppé had been foreign minister. One biographer of Chirac, Philippe Madelin (1998), describes Juppé as 'being passionately in favour of constructing Europe – perhaps with a secret ambition of being elected one day president of a United Europe by universal suffrage'. Juppé saw European monetary union as an essential step towards a common European foreign policy over which France would have considerable sway. Even so, in spring 1992 he had been in no hurry to come off the fence ahead of his boss in favour of the Maastricht Treaty and had even manoeuvred at one point against a constitutional amendment essential to the Treaty's implementation being put through parliament by the Socialist government. Appointed by newly elected President Chirac as prime minister in May 1995, Juppé intended to 'take in hand the president and to straighten out bit by bit some of his heterodox angles'. Juppé shared the anti-'Anglo-Saxon' sentiments of many of the French advocates of monetary union, complaining about the 'gnomes of London' attempting to undermine the *franc fort*.

Juppé, when foreign minister, had introduced to Chirac his head of cabinet, Dominique de Villepin. The new president appointed Villepin as his chief of staff at the Élysée and the three (Chirac, Juppé, and Villepin) became the 'iron trio' of the new administration. The immunity of the president from subsequent criminal prosecution means that a full answer cannot be given to the question of how far the iron link between Chirac and Juppé was forged by co-conspiracy in illicit financing of the Gaullist party. Villepin, a flamboyant aristocrat with some literary talent (later displayed in a biography of Napoleon), is described by Madelin as 'intolerant and dangerously bad-tempered, ... dominated by the charismatic vision of a combative Catholicism, reactionary mysticism, and an elitist conception of politics. Chirac interested him in so far as he could orientate him in the direction of his conservatism.' (All these qualities became world knowledge during the weeks leading up to the spring 2003 war in Iraq, as Villepin, now foreign minister, sought to forge a European and UN strategy to block US action – describing in private the aim as to 'repel Anglo-Saxon liberalism'.) Whilst Villepin got on well with Claude Chirac (the president's daughter), Bernadette Chirac mistrusted his sway over her husband.

The Villepin and Juppé view of France's European policy was of course well in line with the mainstream of thought at the Foreign Office (Quai d'Orsay). The French philosopher André Glucksman describes it as 'Europe must break with the American Empire and become the harbingers of a multi-polarity that balances this super-power. ... The credo of this European power unites the slogans of anti-imperialism and the Communist International of old with the hostile rivalry that the Quai d'Orsay diligently nurtures towards perfidious Albion and the all-pervasive Uncle Sam.' That Villepin and Juppé obtained such influence over Chirac, Madelin explains by 'his attributing to them qualities which he does not possess himself, in particular intellectual virtuosity'. In turn the 'two musketeers' believed that 'an excess of authoritarianism

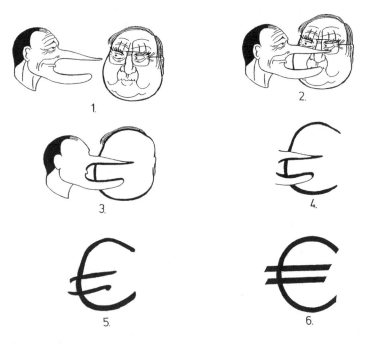

5   How the euro symbol was designed

Source: Hachfeld, *Neues Deutschland*, February 1997.

could compensate for their inexperience and political clumsiness. They are contaminated by the bonapartist appearance of their boss, without the corrective dose of inherent anti-fascism possessed by Chirac.'

The grand vision of France's European policy came up against the reality of clever chess playing by Bonn and Frankfurt. It was with some dismay that President Chirac found himself outmanoeuvred by Bundesbank President Tietmeyer (and most probably at the end of the line by the Chancellor Kohl's office) into being faced with the 'fait accompli' of Dr Duisenberg (who could be counted on to defer to the Bundesbank's chief economist, Otmar Issing) as first president of the ECB rather than a Frenchman. In spring 1998 there was the bizarre spectacle of Chirac pushing for the appointment of Trichet, governor of the Banque de France, as ECB head, even though the prior history of the relationship between the two men was full of rancour. But at that late date no other possible French candidate would have stood a chance. Trichet, as head of the French Treasury from 1987 to 1993, had been intimately involved in all the negotiations between France and Germany leading up to the Maastricht Treaty. He had been a fierce proponent of the strong franc policy from 1987 onwards. And the resolve with which the Socialist government defended the franc's parity against the mark, despite the sharp rise in interest rates required during the German unification boom, was crucial to the EMU train moving forward.

The failures of Karl Otto Pöhl

The role of Trichet, or any other senior economic diplomat and central banker, in driving EMU forward, is surrounded in some ambiguity. All were functionaries in varying degrees. They all had some scope, however, to take a stand out of principle. But they could not be sure, even if that way inclined, that a defiant gesture would alter the path of history significantly. In principle, presidents of the powerful and independent Bundesbank had the most scope to slow or speed up the process of European Monetary Union.

In practice, Karl Otto Pöhl and Hans Tietmeyer, the two long-serving Bundesbank presidents during the last and key stage of the journey to European Monetary Union – from the Franco-German Summit at Evian in June 1988 until the EU Summit ten years later which approved the

January 1999 go-ahead – went along with their political masters, even if grudgingly 'at times. Helmut Schlesinger, Bundesbank president for two years between summer 1991 and summer 1993, did indeed help induce turbulent conditions for the EMU train. But he was not in a position to challenge the pre-set course. Perhaps the previous generation of Bundesbank presidents would have acted differently. In particular it is implausible that the fiercely independent and highly regarded economist predecessor to Pöhl as president, Otmar Emminger, would have put his signature to the Delors Report.

Pöhl and Tietmeyer, unlike previous Bundesbank presidents, had reached the pinnacle via Bonn rather than from within the bank. Pöhl, close to the Social Democrat Party (SPD), had switched career in 1970 from economic journalist to state secretary in the Economics Ministry (following the formation of a SPD-led government under Chancellor Willy Brandt in 1969). Helmut Schmidt, on becoming chancellor (1974), had adopted him as chief economic functionary and diplomat (similar to Kohl's later adoption of Tietmeyer – with the key difference that Schmidt, unlike Kohl, was himself an economist), later installing him in the Bundesbank first as vice-president (1977) and subsequently (January 1980) as president. As vice-president he had helped to smooth the way for the launch of the European monetary system (negotiated between Chancellor Schmidt on the one hand and French Prime Minister Barre together with President Giscard D'Estaing on the other in 1978). Smoothing did not mean conceding. The Emminger-led Bundesbank Council would have no truck with the original Schmidt–Barre draft, under which the independence of German monetary policy might have been compromised. Pöhl himself boasted that the Bundesbank had turned the draft on its head, making the Deutschmark rather than the European currency unit (ecu) the pivot of the new system.

Pöhl had a somewhat softer approach to the subject of European monetary integration than previous Bundesbank presidents – but soft did not mean in any way idealistic or enthusiastic, and there were many ambiguities. For example, on the eve of the new push towards monetary union in spring 1988, Pöhl commented: 'My colleagues and I have publicly argued again and again for years that the aim of European monetary co-operation must be an economic and monetary union – and at the end of this path there must be a European central bank and European currency.' Yet the Bundesbank Annual Report published around the same time concluded that the maintenance of a successful European monetary system would be perfectly adequate to allow the internal market – then under construction following the Single Europe Act – to function smoothly. And in his speeches Pöhl was adamant that the train towards European monetary union should not start until the present European monetary system had expanded to include the UK. (This occurred in autumn 1990 just ahead of the crucial EU Summit in Rome which gave the green light to the start of inter-governmental negotiations leading up to the adoption of the Maastricht Treaty in December 1991.) Pöhl did not elaborate why UK participation in European monetary integration was essential – but on this point he was very close to the position of Helmut Schmidt.

Karl Otto Pöhl had considerable skill in squaring the circle. Yes, monetary union was an acceptable long-run aim once a whole range of prior conditions had been fulfilled (including full UK membership of EMS and abolition of exchange restrictions by France and Italy). In practical terms the start of a formal multi-year process leading up to monetary union would surely be a long time off. Meanwhile it was acceptable to participate constructively in futuristic discussions about the shape of that union long before construction could start, if that is what Bonn required of him. In Pöhl's view it would certainly not be appropriate for the Bundesbank to sabotage discussions.

Nonetheless, Pöhl's relationship to Delors was, at best, cool. The Bundesbank president, a stickler for protocol, resented the lead-role which the EU Commission president was taking in difficult monetary matters where Brussels' competence was at best doubtful. Pöhl was in the end willing to put his signature to the Delors report, having insisted as a condition that it should refer to the need for binding restraints on budget deficits. Pöhl did not, as previous Bundesbank presidents, insist that political should proceed monetary integration. The vice-president under Pöhl, by contrast, Helmut Schlesinger (chief economist and long-time career official at the Bundesbank), continued to remind audiences that German political union in 1871 had preceded monetary union by four years. Yet Pöhl remained close to the established Bundesbank wisdom that economic convergence in Europe should precede monetary union – and thereby opposed to a view popular in Paris that monetary union could come first, acting as a catalyst to economic integration.

Perhaps the train to European Monetary Union would have come to a stop if indeed Pöhl had in the end refused to sign the Delors report (early 1989) and resigned if faced with huge political pressure from Chancellor Kohl to reverse his decision. A year later, a stronger stand by Pöhl might have reduced the ruinous costs (for both East and West) of German monetary union. Instead Pöhl huffed and puffed but then agreed to Hans Tietmeyer, already a member of the Bundesbank Council (since 1989), playing a key role in the detailed design and technical preparation required for replacing the East German currency with the Deutschmark. In the end Chancellor Kohl could credibly claim that the Bundesbank supported his stance on both European and German monetary union.

Counterfactual judgements are notoriously difficult. A bust-up between Pöhl and Kohl could have made political theatre whose final act would have been simply the earlier appointment of Hans Tietmeyer (a Kohl loyalist) as Bundesbank president with no impact on final results. Yet there is an issue of ineffectiveness. Pöhl became an accomplice, albeit reluctant and with some public disagreements along the way, in the pushing forward of two monetary unions (German and European) that were to have a seriously harmful impact on Germany's economic future. The British prime minister at the time, Margaret Thatcher, had based her early anti-EMU strategy on the idea that Pöhl would block the process, without the UK having to exercise its veto, indeed quoting at EU summits a selection of his sceptical remarks. That was a misreading of the Bundesbank president's willingness, skill, or capacity to hold back the tide of monetary integration.

Pöhl's position in negotiations over the shape of monetary union was that the European Central Bank should be modelled on the Bundesbank, independent from governments, and committed constitutionally to the overriding aim of price-level stability. He became mesmerized by the slogan that the new European money should be as stable as the Deutschmark, and indeed made a key contribution to securing that objective. There is no evidence, however, that Pöhl appreciated the considerable burdens which might fall on his country from the sacrifice of its independent stable national money (the Deutschmark), whose exchange rate could be adjusted against other European monies, on the altar of a stable supranational European money. Suppose Germany's high cost base eventually had to fall by international comparison if mass unemployment were to be avoided. How could this take place without deflation if the Deutschmark together with the possibility of devaluation had vanished? Moreover, would a supranational central bank, if created as an ivory-tower institution not embedded in any live political system, be able to follow an effective contra-cyclical policy, albeit subsidiary to the main aim of long-term price stability? Karl Otto Pöhl's dominant assumption that a framework for stability, policed effectively, was the necessary and sufficient condition for European monetary union to work well resonated with the beliefs of the 'monetary nihilists'. (See Chapter 1 for a description of this group of leading central bankers – including Trichet, Duisenberg and Issing.)

Pöhl's deputy, and his successor as Bundesbank President, Helmut Schlesinger, had more perspicacity. He warned of the political catastrophe which could follow from 'concentration on the long term', pointing to the disaster of Brüning's deflationary policies in the years 1930–2 which had culminated in the rise to power of the Nazis. Schlesinger cautioned that it would be wrong to deduce that social peace and political stability could be reached only by abandoning employment and income growth as aims of policy. By the time Schlesinger succeeded Pöhl in summer 1991, the Bundesbank could not suddenly perform a volte-face in its cautious support for European Monetary Union. Moreover Schlesinger's term was only for two years, and his heir-apparent, Hans Tietmeyer, with a direct line to Chancellor Kohl, was now vice-president with special responsibility for international monetary relations.

One trigger to Pöhl's early retirement had been a not-so-private row with Chancellor Kohl over clumsy remarks the president had made in Brussels warning that the disasters of German monetary union should not be repeated at a European level. But the remarks did not have weighty content – other than that there should be no headlong rush into the further monetary union. The backward-looking jibe at the ill-considered nature of German monetary union invited the public response why had the Bundesbank, led by Pöhl, been so accommodative? And indeed Chancellor Kohl in rebuking Pöhl pointed out that the Bundesbank had approved the terms of the monetary union. In any case there were few parallels between the union of ex-communist East Germany to West Germany and European Monetary Union. Why would wages jump in France and Italy following monetary union, as had happened in East Germany? Pöhl denied publicly that disagreement over EMU was a reason for his resignation and David Marsh (1992) in his history of the Bundesbank agrees that the dominant factor was personal – dislike of the tight personal security arrangements and danger of terrorist attack on his family.

Hans Tietmeyer – 'francophile' Kohl loyalist, diplomat and executioner

Indeed the eventual successor to Pöhl as president of the Bundesbank (from September 1993), Hans Tietmeyer, had himself been the subject of a failed assassination attempt when attending (as Kohl's Sherpa) the

Berlin International Monetary Fund meeting in September 1988. Vice-President Tietmeyer was in effect the international face of the Bundesbank under the short presidency of Helmut Schlesinger. He had the reputation of being a francophile and Claude Trichet, as head of the French Treasury and subsequently governor of the Banque de France, at least considered that he had a special line to the Bundesbank via its sympathetic vice-president. Trichet, however, overvalued the significance of this special relationship to Tietmeyer, as became clear during the summer 1993 crisis of the French franc. Tietmeyer was unable or unwilling to lead a revolt against the iron determination of Schlesinger to persevere with monetary tightness even though it might break the ERM link of the franc to the mark. Indeed at the crucial EC meeting convened to discuss the franc crisis on 31 July 1993, Tietmeyer mocked the French delegation with his opening remark that 'this morning I understand we are to speak French' (meaning he had heard through diplomatic channels that Paris would propose that Germany should temporarily float the mark and that the French franc should become the new anchor currency meanwhile of the European Monetary System). The remark was at best inconsistent with the vice-president's francophile reputation.

Tietmeyer was certainly tough. And unlike Trichet he had no romantic or ideological hang-ups about creating Europe. As an Economics Ministry official he had been one of the German delegates in the drawing up of the Werner Report in 1971 – the first blueprint on monetary union in Europe – and had been duly sceptical about the possibility of monetary union preceding political union and full economic convergence. He owed, however, his major career advancements to Chancellor Kohl and was loyal to his objectives for European unity, subject of course to the absolute safeguarding of monetary stability. He was closer to Pöhl than to Schlesinger in down-playing the short-term effectiveness of monetary policy and emphasizing the primacy of the long-run stability framework.

Tietmeyer's emphasis on the long-run framework fitted in some respects with his Jesuit training and deeply Catholic background – coming from a family of eleven children in a small village near the Dutch border. His concern for stability had been crucial to his writing the 'Lambsdorff paper' in 1982, drawing attention to the fundamental deterioration in Germany's public finances and the need for a major tightening of fiscal policy. (Lambsdorff was then the economics minister and co-leader of the Free Democrat Party.) The paper had provided the grounds for the Free Democrats (FDP) pulling out of their coalition with the SPD and joining the CDU under Kohl. Tietmeyer, himself close to the CDU, earned the high respect of the new chancellor, and big career advancements lay ahead.

Understandably, the ex-chancellor, Helmut Schmidt, was no fan of Hans Tietmeyer. In spring 1996 Schmidt published an open letter to Tietmeyer (under the title of 'The Bundesbank – no state within a state' in *Die Zeit* newspaper), in his then position of Bundesbank president, imploring a more positive attitude towards pushing forward European Monetary Union (see Meier, 1997). Schmidt criticized the Bundesbank president for his over-strict interpretation of the budgetary limits established in the Maastricht Treaty as one of the key conditions of eligibility for countries joining EMU. Schmidt also complained that Tietmeyer, by publicly stating monetary union could have serious flaws if there were no progress towards political integration, was turning public opinion against the whole enterprise. Yet its failure could mean a fatal setback to the European integration process, dashing the major strategic aim of German policy from Adenauer to Kohl. Schmidt then questioned the soundness of Tietmeyer's opinions, drawing attention to three serious previous errors of judgement.

First, there was the Lambsdorff paper setting the stage for a new fiscal policy – but since then the public debt had multiplied by four and unemployment reached record levels. Second, Tietmeyer as personal adviser to Kohl (on secondment from the Bundesbank) on monetary union with East Germany had approved a rate of exchange which overvalued the Eastern currency by 100 per cent and directly led to the future economic catastrophe there. Third, Tietmeyer had not pushed for a revaluation of the Deutschmark within the ERM during the period of post-unification monetary squeeze (1991–3) – yet that would have avoided the subsequent ERM crisis of summer 1993 when the narrow-band monetary system broke apart.

The third criticism may be valid in so far as Tietmeyer failed to promote the obvious solution to the monetary and currency tensions in Western Europe during the early 1990s – a temporary revaluation of the mark which would have been reversed once the unification boom had burst and German inflation pressures had dissipated. It may be that senior officials at the Bundesbank gave soft hints to Paris about the desirability of a temporary change in the mark's ERM parities, but the fervent backers there of the strong franc (meaning no devaluation against the mark) would have been studiously deaf. There is no evidence that the subject was ever explicitly discussed between Trichet and Tietmeyer. (The chances of evidence being found even if such a conversation did ever take place would be very low!) In any case, the insistence of the Dutch central bank under Duisenberg on staying at an unchanged parity within a narrow band of fluctuation to the mark would have made it impossible to present a currency realignment as a mark revaluation rather than a franc devaluation. And would the Tietmeyer-led Bundesbank have envisaged canvassing Bonn for a devaluation of the Deutschmark once the German economy entered an economic downturn in the aftermath of the unification boom? Devaluation was a totally taboo topic at the Bundesbank, as at the French Finance Ministry under Finance Minister Bérégovoy and his two monetary 'ayatollahs' (Claude Trichet and Hervé Hannoun). If a later devaluation of the Deutschmark were to be ruled out it was better not to revalue now as a short-term move.

Indeed Tietmeyer's favourite argument in favour of proceeding with European Monetary Union was the benefit of absolute exchange rate stability in the new Europe without frontiers (the completed internal market). In a Mais Lecture delivered in 1998 Tietmeyer stressed that a single currency, above all, makes it possible fully to exploit the economic benefits of integration. The complete transparency of prices would strengthen the forces of competition, and factor allocation would no longer be impaired by exchange rate uncertainty. There would be a fall in exchange-related transaction costs.

Ultimately, there was never any question that the Tietmeyer-led Bundesbank would challenge Chancellor Kohl's headlong rush towards

6   **The first euro**
Source: Chappatte, *Die Weltwoche*, April 1998.

European Monetary Union. And the comments or gestures which Tietmeyer sometimes made suggesting that some delay in the timetable might be necessary were probably no more than bluff tactics towards getting Germany's European partners to make every effort towards reaching the Maastricht convergence criteria. This probably explains the rumours in early 1997 that Tietmeyer was trying to get Holland to propose a delay in the EMU timetable. Indeed, Tietmeyer was masterly in using Holland as a conduit for German policy. In 1993, it was the Dutch link that thwarted the French aim of achieving a temporary exit of the Deutschmark from the ERM and a new role for the franc as anchor currency. (Duisenberg, probably with the pre-knowledge of Tietmeyer, piped up that the florin would remain fixed at an unchanged parity with narrow bands against the Deutschmark, whatever happened.)

In 1996 Tietmeyer prevailed on Duisenberg to put himself forward as a candidate for the next president of the European Monetary Institute (to grow into the ECB), realizing that the Dutchman would defer in monetary policy decision-making to Issing, the likely German member of the ECB board. The Dutch central bank president's academic background had been in econometrics, not monetary economics. He had smothered any ideas of monetary independence in the Netherlands, turning that country into the most steadfast of German monetary satellites (see Chapter 1). Duisenberg was a trusted competent committee chairman (most recently of the EU central bankers' committee) with no strong opinions, and with the good fortune to come from a small country renowned for getting top EU posts. His past as a very moderate social democrat would not cause friction with EU governments of centre-right or left. (Only towards the end of his presidency at the ECB was the anti-US and anti-semitic political orientation of Mrs Duisenberg to become a problem.)

It is not hard to imagine the behind-the-scene manoeuvring by Tietmeyer that brought about the 1996 coup at the European Monetary Institute. Ostensibly the EMI president, Alexandre Lamfalussy, approaching the end of his three-year term (the EMI had opened its doors at the beginning of 1994), called a vote of board members (the chiefs of the EU central banks), without any authorization from the EU Council, to approve Wilhelm Duisenberg as his successor. Lamfalussy, a Hungarian-born Belgian economist and previously president of the Bank for International Settlements was, like Tietmeyer, a grandmaster of European financial diplomacy. Almost certainly the next EMI president would become the first ECB president (a point that Duisenberg had pressed in discussions with Tietmeyer about his candidature).

Trichet – monetary courtesan, ayatollah or dupe?

Why did Claude Trichet, a member of the EMI board, go along with the Tietmeyer–Lamfalussy orchestrated coup? At one level, Trichet may have thought that there was virtually no prospect of President Chirac putting his name forward, given the sourness of the relationship between the two men. Earlier that same year (1996) matters had come to a head when Chirac challenged Trichet, on the occasion of his presenting the annual report of the Banque de France to the president, to explain how the huge losses at the state-owned Crédit Lyonnais could have occurred without the Treasury, where Trichet had been director at the time, sounding the alarm. Trichet's big career steps (head of cabinet at Finance Ministry, 1986, head of Treasury, 1987, governor of the Banque de France, 1993) had occurred under Édouard Balladur, the Gaullist who had challenged Chirac for the presidency in spring 1995. Trichet, sensing at the last minute that the electoral tide had changed in Chirac's favour, had betrayed Balladur by sending an admiring letter to Chirac. In a crucial TV interview, Chirac had pulled the letter out of his pocket and read aloud its contents as evidence of his respectability in the financial world. But Chirac was unhappy with Trichet's obstinacy in refusing to ease monetary policy sharply in summer 1995 at a time of economic weakness. Trichet had delivered the new president an ultimatum. Rate cuts would come only if the new government made deep budget cuts. When these were later announced, the monetary response had been disappointingly timid.

Fiscal austerity was crucial to France meeting the public finance criteria of eligibility for EMU membership as set in the Maastricht target. (The 3 per cent of GDP limit on the general government deficit had indeed been put forward by Trichet in the course of the negotiations between Paris and Bonn leading up to the Treaty – a time when France's budget deficit was small.) Furthermore, Trichet was in firm agreement with Tietmeyer that the big widening in the bands of permitted exchange rate fluctuation (to 15 per cent either side of parity) agreed at the end-July 1993 crisis meeting on the European Monetary System should not become the catalyst to France running an aggressively easy monetary policy and pushing the franc down. Rather monetary policy in the ERM countries, and most importantly France, should be directed at maintaining exchange rates close to their parities. As an enthusiast of European monetary integration, Trichet had no intention of crossing Tietmeyer, whose good will would be essential to the EMU project moving forward particularly in the dangerous period following the virtual breakdown of the exchange rate mechanism in the EMS.

Critics of Trichet have argued that he allowed himself to be manipulated by the diplomatically more skilful Tietmeyer. Indeed Finance Minister Bérégovoy (later briefly prime minister) had been deeply distrustful of Germany in the pre-Maastricht negotiations (1990–1) and feared that Trichet was becoming outmanoeuvred. In the diplomatic game of brinkmanship, the strength of Trichet's European convictions could become a liability. Not that his idealism was totally untarnished by the rough-and-tumble of making it to the top. Critics said that he could be an expert courtesan – as head of Finance Minister Balladur's cabinet in 1986–7 devaluing the franc twice and then becoming the apostle of the strong franc under socialist Finance Minister Bérégovoy from 1998–93. Then, under Prime Minister Balladur, Trichet supported the backstop plan of a temporary float of the Deutschmark and a French-franc anchored ERM.

Nonetheless, as a matter of principle, and in so far as he could abide by this, Trichet was against short-termism in economic policy-making. There is also no record of Trichet advocating any particular design for monetary union on the basis that this would further French influence in the new regime, even though gaining some control over European monetary policy had long been a goal of French governments in their approach to EMU. Could Trichet not have proposed a structure at the ECB where the chairman of the policy-making committee (as distinct from the bank president) would be the governor of one of largest three member central banks (Bundesbank, Banque de France and Banca d'Italia) in rotation? That would have had some similarity with the pre-1933 Federal Reserve system where the president of the New York Federal Reserve Bank was the chairman of the open-market committee.

Aeschman and Riché (1999), in drawing their character portrait of Trichet, comment that

> the common denominator of his intuitions is the long term. His favourite words and phrases are revealing – perserverance, mission, equilibrium. For him the French economy is chained by traditions, corporatisms, and archaisms. These will take time to break down – and a strong franc and later a hard EURO will help in that long-run task. He decrees as an axiom that European Monetary Union will take place because it is inscribed in a fundamental historical process. For Trichet Europe is before all else to do with values and culture – menaced by Americanization. Without European integration, these

values would get lost in the great American bath. To make the single European currency is to preserve the values and strengthen the identity of Western Europe... perhaps also it might safeguard his garden of poetry – Goethe, Véronése – which he loved so much.

(Trichet was the only European central banker ever to appear on a TV programme about poetry and with him reading his favourites!)

The decisive contribution which Claude Trichet made as functionary to keeping the EMU train on track was his persuading Prime Minister Balladur in summer 1993 against a unilateral bold easing of French monetary policy and piling the pressure on the new Chirac administration in 1995 to meet the Maastricht criteria. A central bank chief with greater democratic sensitivities, and inclined to put more weight on the short-term aim of helping to stimulate a recovery of the French economy, might well have cut rates sharply, leaving fiscal policy and any implications for the pace of the journey to EMU to be resolved by the government. He would not have threatened to raise rates or delay rate cuts (as the case may be) if the franc fell due to the government failing to pursue the Maastricht fiscal target vigorously.

Perhaps the trio of Chirac, Villepin and Juppé would have decided on a safe journey to EMU as their overriding aim, irrespective of who was at the head of the Banque de France, but no counterfactual proof is possible. Chirac might have wavered. In monetary history – as in any other area of history – defining the contribution of persons as against powerful underlying forces is a non-exact science. And so it is with the history of the strong franc. Would Finance Minister Bérégovoy have found someone other than Trichet (as senior Finance Ministry official) to steer through his policy of pursuing unswervingly the hard franc? Most probably yes, but there was the possibility that another person in that role would have persuaded the finance minister, who always had some doubts, on the merits of an alternative course. Even so, was the strong franc policy essential to achieving monetary union? The events following the ERM virtual break-up of summer 1993 suggest that monetary union could be achieved without exchange rate fluctuations being held continuously within tight bands around an unchanged parity.

A round-up of the functionaries

High functionaries can affect the course of events not just through actual decisions taken but also by decisions or courses of action not taken. We have seen how Karl Otto Pöhl affected the form of monetary union by his insistence on political independence of the central bank and the absolute primacy of the target for low inflation. Pöhl – and indeed his colleagues on the Delors committee – failed to imagine a world where inflation was virtually dead and the key issues for monetary policy might be combating deflation and providing economic stimulus. And they did not contemplate the large relative price level adjustments that might be required over time between member countries in a monetary union nor the particular difficulty in achieving these where there is no significant overall inflation. There is a missing chapter in the monetary section of the Maastricht Treaty – no spelling out of the central bank's policy aims beyond price level stability, and no framework for compelling pre-emptive action against deflation. In any case, by Pöhl signing the Delors report, the Bundesbank became a sponsor, however unenthusiastic, of European Monetary Union.

Pöhl's successor (after the short interlude of Helmut Schlesinger), Hans Tietmeyer, was a skilled co-driver of the EMU train. Kohl was in the front seat – but Tietmeyer's continuing show of Bundesbank hardness, vetting, and ultimate approval was crucial to winning the confidence of German households and businesses in the new monetary order. Moreover, another Bundesbank president might have made less effort to keep the EMU train going after the ERM crisis of summer 1993. His diplomacy was successful in getting Germany's preferred candidate installed as the first ECB president. But Tietmeyer had no more perspicacity than had Pöhl when it came to drafting detailed rules for the implementation of monetary policy by the European Central Bank. So long as the goal of low inflation was enshrined – and strong barriers placed in the way of excess budgetary deficits – then all should be well with the new monetary union and with Germany. Tietmeyer, no more than Pöhl, saw any need to press for safeguards that Germany would indeed carry weight in future European monetary policy-making.

In particular, neither Pöhl nor Tietmeyer made any protest against the politically correct proposal of one national central bank president one vote – the same for Luxembourg as for Germany. Perhaps they could not imagine the situation where one day a future chancellor would be swayed by political considerations to appoint a mediocre candidate as head of the Bundesbank to whom the rest of the ECB Council would pay scant attention. Yet that is what happened in spring 1999 when the recently elected Chancellor Schröder on the recommendation of his finance minister, Hans Eichel, appointed Ernst Welteke as successor to Hans Tietmeyer as Bundesbank president. Welteke had been economics minister in the Hesse regional government (dominated by the SPD) before being appointed by the then SPD prime minister of Hesse, Hans Eichel, to be head of the Hesse central bank (and thereby as a regional central bank president to membership of the Bundesbank Council). Eichel himself had been appointed as finance minister in the federal government only in early 1999, following the sudden resignation of Oskar Lafontaine.

If the central bank's policy-making was not to extend beyond preserving price stability, and indeed Germany and France were always near the average inflation performance for the euro-area as a whole, vote-weighting in the ECB council and the stature of the Bundesbank president were not decisive issues. Pöhl and Tietmeyer did not contemplate seriously the ECB having to use counter-cyclical monetary policy in conditions where the severity of the potential economic downturn varied across the euro-area and with the German economy at one extreme rather than in the centre. Then the optimum monetary policy for Germany might be significantly different from that for the other countries in the union. What would be the mechanism for compromise? Would Germany's interests be best served by leaving policy in such circumstances to be determined on an entirely discretionary basis by an ivory tower of eurocrat central bankers? The failure to consider – and address – that issue could ultimately pose an existential threat to the euro.

3
Separation and Dissolution

There is nothing in the Treaty of Maastricht about how countries can withdraw from European monetary union. Indeed, a withdrawal would be a breach of the Treaty. But broken treaties are the subject matter of much history! Past experience of monetary unions suggest that they do disintegrate. The very different nature, however, of today's European monetary union from previous smaller unions founded under the gold or bimetallic standards limits seriously the value of studying past episodes.

As a matter of fact, none of the negotiating parties setting up European monetary union put forward a proposal for there to be a set of clauses dealing with individual countries exiting or with a total break-up. They may have done so if monetary union was to be an experimental arrangement. As illustration, the would-be members could have agreed a ten-year union with renewal to be non-binding on any party. Proceedings for separation of individual members or dissolution of the whole would have been laid out at the start. In practice, however, the main negotiating parties (with the exception of those who decided not to join) saw monetary union as a key irreversible step in the process of European economic and political integration, not as a monetary experiment.

For Chancellor Kohl, a principal argument for monetary union was that it would establish permanent peace between member countries. Why, then, would Germany seek to insert a dissolution and separation chapter in the Treaty that might only weaken its peace-making power? And it is surely unlikely that President Mitterrand would have won a referendum to approve a softer style Maastricht Treaty in which monetary union was drafted in the form of a ten-year monetary experiment. By admitting that union could be a mistake and spelling out the inevitable costly procedures for dissolution, the pro-EMU advocates would have almost certainly weakened their case. (The exception would have been with respect to a surely very small minority of citizens who might have been persuaded to give monetary union a trial but not irrevocable approval.) Moreover, a key selling point of monetary union in the French referendum was that it would help contain the power of the newly united Germany. That would hardly be the case if Germany could simply decide not to re-contract into monetary union at the end of ten years.

There is no evidence, in any case, that the principal founders ever considered seriously the possibility of the union breaking up or shrinking. And none of the leading functionaries were inclined to fill in the details. Preparing texts on contingency arrangements for separation and dissolution would have jarred with the main selling theme for EMU, especially in the Brussels propaganda hand-outs. In this, monetary integration would play a crucial role in furthering the development of the European single market for goods and services. Yes, the UK had obtained an opt-out from the union. But if EMU became a club from which entry and exits could occur at will, then the single market would come into question. And already in 1995 the sharp depreciation of the Italian lira in the wake of the Mexico crisis had brought talk (not more than that!) of possible French-led action against cheap Italian imports. In any event, the leading functionaries would not have been rewarded in any way for contemplating scenarios of separation or dissolution and bringing these to the notice of their political masters! If indeed a present member decided in the future to pull out of the union, or all members resolved that the union should be dissolved, then an inter-governmental separation or dissolution agreement would presumably have to be drawn up from scratch. The EU Commission would probably play an important role in the drafting process. In some scenarios, the agreement would follow the initial act of separation.

In turn the Commission proposals would be the subject of negotiations between the various sovereign governments. That may well be an advantage for all compared to negotiations constrained by an ill-constructed separation and dissolution chapter in the Maastricht Treaty. The ideal, however, might well have been an enunciation of general principles. These would have included guidelines as to how to deal with euro banknotes in the event of dissolution of the whole union. Specific obligations would also be set out for the case of one member leaving the union which otherwise remains intact. In particular, the responsibility would be set out of the exiting member to redeem euro banknotes that had previously circulated domestically as the principal form of cash. In addition, there might be a general ruling that forced conversions of deposits and loans into a new national money in the event of exit should apply only to residents, not non-residents (an economic rationale for this last rule is given in the example below of a sudden withdrawal by Holland).

Disintegration scenarios for monetary union

It is possible to map out a number of different scenarios for EMU break-up – partial or whole.

First, there are various types of forced exits. A country might break the fundamental rules for EU membership (for example, concerning human rights and democracy). It is not possible for a country to remain part of EMU once expelled from the EU. Alternatively, a country might become engulfed in a financial crisis for which the only remedy is the re-institution of a national money printing press. Examples include a severe banking crisis (in one member country) in which the ECB would not have the authority to lend sufficient funds to restore calm and where the national government would lack the credit status to make an emergency issue of bonds to provide aid. Or a newly elected government in one member country might decide to openly flout the Treaty limits on budget deficits, refuse to pay fines (for budget excesses), and experience a debt crisis (as the prices of government bonds collapse). No rescue in such circumstances would come from the ECB. Or a member country might find itself at war with a non-member country (leading to a financial crisis in which the ECB could not act as lender of last resort).

Second, there are the strategic exits. A mainstream political party in one of the member countries might put forward the view that the national economy is suffering from EMU membership and a more prosperous future lies outside. And that party might eventually come into government. A variant of this scenario is where the euro-area as a whole falls into a deflationary depression. Any one country might make a quick escape by pulling out of EMU and devaluing its new currency versus the euro. Another variant is where the ECB makes a major policy mistake and submerges the union in a high inflation. Then there is resistance to a rapid correction. An individual country might decide to move back to stability more quickly – introducing its own money and revaluing it against the euro. Finally there is the democratic choice of a member country to withdraw from the EU. A government elected on a programme of pulling out of the EU would have to negotiate an exit from EMU as part of the withdrawal process.

In general, a forced exit or a strategic decision to withdraw by one country can have contagious effects on other members. A smaller union might be less attractive than the present to several if not all members. In particular, a potential withdrawal by Germany might trigger dissolution, as several countries would rather revert to having their own national monies than remain part of a severely truncated union. Dissolution of the whole would almost always involve more complex intergovernmental negotiation than individual separation.

Lessons from the break-up of the Austro-Hungarian union

History provides only one serious guide to how a monetary union not based on gold or silver breaks up. The falling apart of the Austro-Hungarian political and monetary union after World War I (the crown's link to gold had been broken at the outbreak of the conflict in 1914) has some relevance to a potential separation or dissolution crisis in the European Monetary Union. But this example is an historical extreme.

The issue of what to do about an overhang of banknotes and debt in the defunct or shrunken common currency was important in the case of Austria-Hungary and would be for EMU. But the successor countries of the Austro-Hungarian countries after the collapse of the Hapsburg empire were bent on nationalistic courses and had no inclination to negotiate an orderly transition. The governments of the newly independent peoples (Czechs, Slovaks, Yugoslavs) strove to take on as little of the debt and currency legacy from the hated dual monarchy (in which Austria and Hungary together enjoyed political hegemony). The overriding issue on which negotiations could not be avoided was what to do about the huge total of government debt left behind by the defunct empire (most of which had been issued to finance wartime expenditure) and held widely by investors (including banks) in all the successor countries.

The old currency, the Austro-Hungarian currency, did live on for several years after the death of the Austro-Hungarian political and monetary union, its domain shrinking as each of the successor governments introduced new monies (see Brown, 1986; Rasin, 1923; Garber and Spencer, 1994). Czechoslovakia was the first to act, sealing its frontiers for several days as all Austro-Hungarian banknotes held by residents of the newly independent country were stamped. The stamped notes served as the new Czech currency until new notes could be printed. The other countries followed, last of all Hungary.

Eventually the Austro-Hungarian banknotes expired almost worthless, having enjoyed some brief respite due to conversion operations by Italy in its new territories (Trentino and Trieste) acquired from the vanquished Hapsburg empire. Forgers also played an important role by turning unstamped notes into stamped (such operations were no longer feasible once the successor countries replaced stamped notes with their own newly printed notes). The terms of final liquidation (of the Austro-Hungarian central bank and its banknotes) were determined eventually by the wartime Allies.

The hypothetical example of Quebec separating from Canada

Any separation from or dissolution of the European Monetary Union would take place in a vastly different economic, political, and technical context from that of Austria-Hungary. A nearer guide comes from the tentative discussions in Canada about the currency consequences of a hypothetical independence of Quebec. The issue became live during the close 1994 referendum in Quebec on withdrawal from Canada. The separatists did not spell out in detail the monetary side of a divorce from English-speaking Canada. Indeed, the referendum was on the question of whether the government should open negotiations on separation with Ottawa rather than on the final settlement proposals.

The presumption, which the separatists encouraged, was that an independent Quebec would try to negotiate a monetary union and possibly a new political union with English-speaking Canada. (The monetary union would involve the creation of a Canada–Quebec central bank with a well-defined independence from and accountability to the political authorities in both countries.) If that failed, however, Quebec might switch to using the US dollar. It was unlikely, though, that Washington would facilitate US dollarization (by empowering the Federal Reserve to provide lender of last resort facilities to Quebec banks) unless English-speaking Canada co-operated and Quebec were ready to accept US supervision of its banking system. Even then, there was the obstacle of the US Treasury being fundamentally hostile to dollarization in Latin America – and so how could an exception be justified in North America?

It would have been possible of course for an independent Quebec to continue using the Canadian currency during an interim period of several years until either a monetary union could be agreed or a decision in favour of US dollarization were taken. Quebec's continuing use of the Canadian dollar, now the currency of English-speaking Canada, could be described as Canadian dollarization. No doubt a newly independent

Quebec would have tried to persuade Ottawa that the Bank of Canada should continue to act as lender of last resort (providing emergency injection of funds in any liquidity crisis) to Quebec banks during the interim period. In return Quebec would have had to concede that Ottawa remain in control of financial supervision and regulation. How much goodwill would exist on either side towards easing the process of separation would depend on the thorny question as to what proportion of federal government debt outstanding (on the date of splitting up) Quebec would take over as its own.

Ultimately, if negotiations between Quebec and Ottawa on monetary union and then between Quebec and Washington on US dollarization failed, then an independent Quebec might have launched its own currency rather than persevere with Canadian dollarization. In practice, there was no discussion during the referendum campaign about the technicalities or principles of how and in what form (fixed exchange rate or floating?) a Quebec currency would have been launched. A starting-point would have been the creation of a central bank in Quebec responsible for clearing funds in Canadian dollars between banks in the newly independent country. (Indeed, also under the scenarios of long-term dollarization, either in Canadian or US form, a Quebec interbank clearing institute would be established eventually.) In turn Quebec banks would have been required to hold their reserves against Canadian dollar deposits with the Quebec central bank rather than with the Bank of Canada. (In turn the Quebec central bank would have clearing arrangements with the Bank of Canada. All of this would be the subject of negotiations between Quebec and Ottawa.) Then the ultimate currency divorce could have taken one of the forms – slow or quick – described below for the hypothetical case of European monetary disintegration.

An illustration of a slow staged withdrawal from EMU

The nearest counterpart to the Quebec discussion in the European context might be a potential exit of the UK from the EU. Suppose that at some point in the next few years the UK were to join the European Monetary Union. But then a new wave of anti-EU sentiment sweeps the UK, intensified perhaps by disillusion with EMU membership. One of the major parties adopts EU withdrawal in its programme, subject to referendum approval. If that referendum were to subsequently take place, the advocates of withdrawal would surely have to sketch the monetary consequences. The main differences from the Quebec illustration are, first, the EU is not a federal political entity but a loose political association of sovereign states. Second, in consequence, there is a much smaller issue of what to do about outstanding debt in the name of the now defunct or truncated political union. The share of Canada's federal government debt that an independent Quebec should take over is much larger relative to economic size (of Quebec or English-speaking Canada) than debt issued in the name of the EU relative to the size of the UK or the rest of the EU.

The smoothest exit procedure for the UK from EMU and the EU would be a phased withdrawal. There would be a period of years during which the UK remained a member of EMU, or at least continued to use the euro and enjoy certain privileges. (An important issue would be the ECB continuing to offer joint assistance with the Bank of England as lender of last resort to London-based banks in the event of a financial crisis.) Suppose the UK government in early 2021 obtained a yes vote in a referendum on EU withdrawal, and negotiated by mid-2022 a treaty whereby exit from the EU and cessation of any privileges at the ECB were to take final effect at the end of 2025. As soon as 2023 the UK could make a start on issuing its own currency again. The phasing in of the pound would follow in reverse order its phasing out to make way for the euro.

There would be a first stage during which the Bank of England stood ready to convert euro deposits with itself (held by banks) into pounds or conversely at a 1 : 1 rate. Pounds would not yet be introduced in the form of cash (banknotes or coin). Legislation would be enacted so that government offices (including tax offices) and regulated public utilities would have to accept pounds or euros on a 1 : 1 basis (during Stage 1). Most businesses would follow suit, but there would be no compulsion. Legislation would also stipulate that UK resident clients of banks could freely decide what proportion of their deposits or loans to switch from euros into pound denomination (non-resident conversions could also take place, but only by agreement between the bank and its client). In the debt markets, private sector issuers could use the new currency as denominator of loans. The UK government would make all new debt issues in pound denomination and be ready to convert any bonds held by the Bank of England into pounds on a 1 : 1 basis.

Technically, interest rates could vary on pounds and euros during the first stage just described. In principle and practice, however, there would only be significant differentials in the case of bonds or deposits whose maturity lay in Stage 2 (where absolute 1 : 1 convertibility would no longer apply) and beyond. Short-maturity pound and euro bonds and deposits would be virtually perfect substitutes and so their interest rates could not diverge significantly. As the second stage approached, the maturities for which divergent interest rates could appear would become progressively shorter. A key determinant of interest rate spreads would be expectations as regards the UK pound/euro exchange rate through Stage 2 and beyond. For example, expectations that the pound would fall below parity with the euro would be reflected in long-term pound interest rates being above euro equivalents. The separation process would operate most smoothly if there were no strong directional expectations – the best guess being that the pound would trade around parity in Stage 2 (albeit with some volatility).

Stage 2 could run from say mid-2025 to end 2026 (overlapping exit from the EU at end-2025). On say, 1 July 2025, the Bank of England would suspend 1:1 convertibility between euro and pound deposits with itself – according to the plan already announced at the start of Stage 1. A spot UK pound/euro exchange market would come into existence (until this point, through Stage 1, only a forward exchange market with delivery dates into Stage 2 and beyond would function). The UK pound/euro rate would now be determined by market forces, but throughout Stage 2 a fixed-exchange rate system would be in operation. The pound/euro rate would be free to fluctuate within a band either side of parity (taken as £/euro = 1). A notional starting width of 2.5 per cent (5 per cent in total) might be specified already in 2023. Both the parity level and the width of the band would be subject to review. From the start of Stage 2 (mid-2025) the Bank of England would be ready to issue pound banknotes on a 1:1 basis against pound deposits with itself.

There would be a seigniorage agreement with the remaining countries in EMU whereby the Bank of England would buy (against euro deposits) the euro banknotes that would accumulate in their central bank coffers as a consequence of UK residents disposing of them in exchange for the new pound banknotes. (Seigniorage is the revenue that a government derives from the issue of banknotes or non-interest bearing deposits by the central bank.) Otherwise the dumping of euro banknotes by UK residents would erode seigniorage which the remaining governments in EMU derived from banknote issue. And there could be some modest downward strain on the euro as the UK on a net basis obtained a direct transfer of resources from the euro area over the medium term equal to the disposal of notes. (Total euro banknotes in circulation amounted to around 5 per cent of euro-area GDP in 2003.)

Dumping would occur mainly in the form of UK residents depositing euro banknotes in exchange for euro deposits and then selling the euro deposits in the currency markets in exchange for pounds. The banks receiving the euro banknotes would exchange them at union member central banks for euro reserves. The latter (union member central banks – no longer including the Bank of England) would have to sell bonds to mop up the extra reserves created – otherwise inflation pressure would build up – and in doing so their government's seigniorage would be reduced. (In the union member central bank balance sheets, holdings of euro banknotes emanating from the UK would replace some government bond holdings.) The UK government's willingness to negotiate a seigniorage agreement would be influenced, of course, by the extent of good will between itself and the EU – and one element here would be the extent of co-operation of Brussels in easing the UK's withdrawal.

The introduction of sterling banknotes would coincide with the government (including local governments) switching to set all tax demands in pounds only. Social welfare payments would be redenominated and paid in pounds. All public sector prices and public utility rates would be set in pounds – and so would public sector wages. But retail payments to public sector entitities and utilities could still be made in euro cash during a transitional period of, say, one year, with the amount due being converted from pounds into euros on the basis of the latest official exchange rate (an average market rate set on a daily or weekly basis). Legislation would provide for dual pricing in the retail sector of the UK economy during the same transitional period and customers could pay in pound or euro banknotes. Prices would be quoted in both euros and UK pounds, with the implicit exchange rate being the latest reference exchange rate (the state of information technology two decades from now should surely allow for dual pricing at little cost!). After the end of the transitional period there would be no legal requirement for retailers to display prices in euros (alongside pound prices). Whether dual pricing would continue would be left to market forces.

All outstanding UK government debt still in euro denomination would be converted into pounds at a 1 : 1 rate at the start of Stage 2. Private debts would not be subject to any forced conversion from euros into pounds. Borrowers and lenders would freely decide on what action to take in the marketplace (largely the swap markets) to change the currency mix of their liabilities and assets. In the private sector it would be a matter of choice whether wages should be negotiated and settled in pounds or euros. All rental agreements applying to property situated in the UK would be converted into pounds on a 1 : 1 basis from the start of Stage 2, unless both landlord and tenant agreed to maintain euro denomination. All public sector bodies and public utilities would insist on pound denomination in rental agreements to which they are a party (either as tenant or landlord).

There would be no rush to convert euro into pound banknotes under these provisions on day 1 of Stage 2. The euro would still serve as a usable medium of exchange. A main immediate determinant of the pound/euro exchange rate would be the extent of asymmetry between investment and borrower demand for the new currency, already evident in the last months of Stage 1. Some demand for pounds on the eve of Stage 2 would come from bank clients preparing to draw the new notes and coin (available on day 1 against pound deposits). But this demand would be offset by the prospective buying of euros (against the sale of pounds) by the Bank of England as part of the seigniorage agreement with the remaining member countries in EMU.

On balance, suppose that banks were to find many more loans than deposits (in total size) being converted into pounds ahead of Stage 2. (Once Stage 2 starts, conversion is no longer on a 1:1 basis but via currency transactions at the market rate – a reason why most UK bank clients would switch significant proportions of their assets and liabilities from euros into pounds before Stage 1 ends.) Banks cannot carry significant exchange risk and so in the late days of Stage 1 they would seek to close their potential exposure to a rise in the £/euro rate (depreciation of the pound) by various hedging transactions. For example, the banks could sell pounds forward against euros or equivalently borrow pounds and lend euros with maturity dates extending into Stage 2. They would be careful to protect themselves against a discontinuous fall in the immediate transition from Stage 1 to Stage 2 and against any violent short-term interest rate fluctuations on the pound around the same time.

Indeed, pound interest rates for short periods straddling the end of Stage 1 and the beginning of Stage 2 could rise to sky-high levels under the pressure of hedging transactions. (These high rates would be consistent with a consensus view that the newly independent pound would drop towards the low end of its band against the euro right from the start.) Interest rates (on pounds) would taper off for long maturities, given the strong expectation that the Bank of England would aim for a normal level of interest rates on its newly independent currency. Indeed, the sharp fall in interest rates would be the immediate trigger to the pound's early decline.

If pound banknotes were to be issued during Stage 1 there would be huge waves of these back into bank deposits in the days running up to the start of Stage 2 under the scenario of high short-term interest rates and a consensus view that the pound would be weak. Prior holders would dump them in exchange for euro banknotes or high-interest short-term pound deposits over the transition from Stage 1 to 2. Banks would bear a high and volatile interest cost on their swollen holdings of pound cash (either banknotes or overnight deposits at the Bank of England). The non-issue of pound banknotes until the start of Stage 2 would avoid this possible problem. (There is no problem if the pound is expected to be neither strong nor weak.)

By contrast, if in the run-up to Stage 2 banks were to find their deposits in pound denomination growing faster than their loans, their hedging operations might cause interest rates for short periods straddling the transition between the two stages to fall to substantially negative levels. The absence of any banknotes in the new currency eliminates the main barrier to sub-zero interest rates (otherwise depositors would simply pull funds out of the banks and hold cash under the mattress). The other possible barrier is positive or zero interest being paid by the central bank on deposits placed with it. This can be eliminated by the central bank paying a market-related rate (negative in this case).

Indeed, if pound banknotes were to be available in Stage 1 and pound bank deposits at the Bank of England subject to a zero-interest rate floor, then under these conditions (potential excess demand for pounds at the 1 : 1 exchange rate) there could be grave instability. Clients would seek to hoard pound banknotes rather than suffer negative rates of interest. In response, UK banks would scramble to liquidate euro assets and convert the euro cash obtained into pounds on the basis of 1 : 1 at the Bank of England. Those operations might well strain the euro-system as a whole. The ECB might be forced to provide massive injections of liquidity so as to prevent a financial crisis erupting throughout the euro-area.

The existence of negative interest rates on the pound (for periods straddling the end of Stage 1 and start of Stage 2) would be consistent with the newly independent currency jumping towards the top of its new permitted range of fluctuation against the euro as soon as Stage 2 started (at which point interest rates would spring through the zero barrier). One factor behind greater investor than borrower demand for the pound in the run-up to Stage 2 might be a negative view of the euro – perhaps due to a very pessimistic economic assessment of the core European economies. Another might be the behaviour of pension funds. If legislation provided that some part of private pension payments were to be converted 1 : 1 into pounds at the start of Stage 2, then these would have to switch a huge volume of funds out of euros (or sell euros forward against pounds) to hedge the new exchange risk – and these operations would proceed during Stage 1.

During Stage 2, given the primacy of the exchange rate target, there would be no great scope as yet for an independent monetary policy by the Bank of England, despite its full withdrawal from the European System of Central Banks. In any case, huge uncertainty as to the demand for pound-denominated money, related to the unpredictability of how quickly and to what extent the new money would take over from the old, would make any traditional guidelines to an independent policy unreliable. For Stage 3, the final phase of regained monetary independence for the UK, starting at the end of 2026, a credible framework for monetary stability would have to be set out.

Most probably the framework would be based on a joint system of inflation and monetary targets, providing for flexibility in the event of severe business cycle fluctuations. There would be rules regarding accountability to the public and to parliament whilst maintaining political independence. The framework might also include some system of automatic triggers to pre-emptive action in the face of climbing deflation risks and also for government central bank co-operation in the event of the economy falling into a deflationary depression. The presumption would be that the fixed-exchange rate regime for the pound would be phased out – either all at once or by way of a widening of the bands of permitted fluctuation.

The new pound regime to which the UK would return in the above example has some dissimilarities with the pre-EMU regime. First, there is the simple – and unimportant – arithmetic point that the new pound is set equal to 1 euro at the start as against the old pound in a range of say around 0.70 euro/£. That does not mean that the pound has been devalued during the period of EMU membership but that it is a totally new currency. Second, the new pound would probably be less pervasive in use than the old. There would still be a large overhang of euro liabilities and assets left over from the period of EMU membership that investors or borrowers had decided not to convert into pounds or hedge, as the case may be. In some sectors of the UK economy, the euro might still live on (especially those highly geared to exports) for the purpose of denominating prices and even wages.

The whole procedure of recreating a new pound monetary order and exiting from EMU would carry costs. The biggest cost would be loss of economic growth resulting from a raised level of monetary uncertainty in the late months of Stage 1 and through most of Stage 2. Less important, but nonetheless significant, would be conversion and risk management costs incurred in the banking sector. In addition, households would have to bear the inconvenience of adjusting their investment and liability portfolios to the new monetary regime. The putting of the public sector and utilities at the vanguard of the invading monetary order against the retreating euro regime could raise certain questions of social justice.

The total economic costs of regime change – from EMU back to an independent pound – can be compared with prospective economic benefits. If there is a net gain then there is no monetary cost to withdrawal from the EU. If there is a net loss, then that has to be weighed against any wider economic or political advantages for the UK from pulling out of the EU. But the sketch just given of how withdrawal from EMU could occur shows that the process is indeed feasible. The same would be true of a withdrawal of the UK from EMU but not from the EU (if indeed the other EU partners were to agree to this). The procedure would be the same – but the cost–benefit analysis justifying it would not include notional political gains from EU withdrawal.

The scientific analogy is that a country withdrawing from EMU has to separate its currency from the euro solution formed out of the original sovereign monies. The separation process is not costless but it is certainly feasible. Some advocates of EMU would have us believe that European monetary integration is like a chemically irreversible change – scrambling an egg that cannot be subsequently unscrambled. That is not true.

A rapid strategic exit to escape deflation or inflation

The same analogy would apply to our next hypothetical example of a strategic (rather than forced) decision by a member country to exit from EMU so as to escape from a deflationary depression engulfing the euro-area. The main differences from the UK example above are first, withdrawal is to occur quickly (not over several years) in order to overcome serious present economic difficulties, and, second, it is evident that the new currency will be devalued against the euro right at the start of its existence.

For purposes of illustration, suppose that the Dutch government decides that it will lift the Netherlands economy out of a euro-area wide deflationary depression by introducing its own currency at a cheap rate against the euro. This decision would not come out of the blue. Most probably there would have been months of speculation amidst heated political debate. During that time a large 'Holland premium' might well have appeared on euro interest rates quoted by Dutch banks and on Dutch government bond yields relative to the prevailing level elsewhere in the euro-area. The premium would reflect the danger that EMU-exit could take place suddenly and by way of a forced 1:1 conversion of euro deposits and loans with Dutch banks and of Dutch government bonds into the new devalued currency (florins).

This sharp rise in Dutch interest rates could bring some economic dislocation. There could be a severe loss of international borrowing and loan business for Dutch banks unless it were 100 per cent certain that forced conversion would apply only to resident euro deposits and loans. (But who in the Netherlands would be able to give that assurance to non-residents? There would be less danger of crisis if EMU members had already formally agreed amongst themselves by way of treaty that non-resident deposits or loans would be exempt from any forced conversions in the event of an exit from EMU.) Non-residents of Holland would in general not wish to be involved in the risk-return calculation of balancing higher interest rates against unknown devaluation risks and simply move their banking business elsewhere in the meantime.

Dutch residents, by contrast, are less exposed to risk because devaluation would not push the domestic price level up in the same proportion as the discount on the new currency versus the euro. Moreover they are likely to have strong convenience and relationship ties to their local banks. During the period of monetary regime uncertainty, however, Dutch residents would be looking at a level of real interest rates considerably higher than normal. Nominal rates in the Netherlands would include a premium reflecting the possible depreciation. But the potential jump in the Dutch price level would be less than the depreciation. The high real rates would be good news for holders of savings deposits, but not for borrowers.

Even so, Dutch savers would choose to move some of their euro deposits abroad (at the cost of less interest income) so as to hedge the risk of a bigger or sooner jump in the domestic price level (after devaluation) than discounted by the raised level of Dutch money rates. Some Dutch borrowers would move part of their borrowing to foreign banks on a speculative view that they could cut their interest costs by more than any eventual loss from the euro rising in value versus a yet-to-be-created sovereign Dutch currency.

If the technical apparatus already exists for separating resident and non-resident accounts, and there is a firm basis for believing that non-resident accounts will not be subject to forced conversion, then the dislocation caused by EMU-exit speculation should be somewhat less than otherwise. Banks in the Netherlands should not lose non-resident business if this is insulated from currency risk. Indeed, they would be able to attract additional non-resident euro deposits (at perhaps only a very slight margin above the going rate in the rest of the euro-area) to fund any gap created by domestic savers switching to banks outside the Netherlands at a faster pace than domestic borrowers. (A net liability position, however, in non-resident business exposes the Dutch banks to loss in the event of an exit from EMU. Banks in funding a net with-drawal of domestic funds by foreign borrowing would gain on interest income account but at the cost of increased risk-bearing.)

Nonetheless, under some circumstances, for example a sharp rise in domestic euro rates (in the Netherlands) and a resulting threat of finan-cial crisis, the Dutch government might have no practical alternative to proceeding with a forced exit from EMU. This might occur even before the formalities could be completed of a referendum or parliamentary vote. If so, the government might seek to present the forced exit as tem-porary, with a re-entry feasible if the vote went against withdrawal from EMU. Otherwise the government might be accused by the political opposition of acting without due concern for democratic choice.

Whether forced or not, the means of making a quick exit from EMU would be for the Dutch central bank to block the transfer of euro deposits held by Dutch banks with itself to other central banks in the European System of Central Banks (ESCB). The blocking would not apply to that share of euro deposits with itself which represents reserves against non-resident euro business for each bank. As illustration, if non-resident deposits in euros with Dutch bank A represented 20 per cent of its total euro deposits, then 20 per cent of its reserves with the Dutch central bank would remain in euros, still freely transferable into the clearing system amongst EMU central banks.

Immediately following the blocking action, Dutch banks could no longer undertake to make payments in euros on behalf of residents out of their existing euro accounts to recipients in other euro-area countries or into non-resident euro accounts in Holland. The order that accom-panied the central bank action would specify that all payments (in the clearing system but not yet complete) before the shock announcement would be honoured. Dutch banks would have to create immediately a new currency category 'Dutch euros', and all resident deposits in euros would be labelled accordingly. They (the banks) would be ready to transfer monies freely on a 1 : 1 basis between 'Dutch euro' accounts.

The 'Dutch euro' reserves held by Dutch banks at the central bank could be used in clearing operations between the Dutch banks – meaning that the domestic payments system would continue to function without break. A central bank or government order would stipulate that

Dutch resident borrowers could use 'Dutch euros' in settlement of loans outstanding from Dutch banks. In effect, loans to Dutch residents by Dutch banks would be redenominated as 'Dutch euro' (rather than 'euro'). A new category of account would be opened for non-residents – in addition to euro deposits (which would remain freely transferable at 1 : 1 for payments to other euro-area countries) they could hold 'Dutch euro' accounts (into which payments could be received from 'Dutch euro' accounts held by Dutch residents and from which payments could be made only into other 'Dutch euro' accounts). And there would be a new category of account for Dutch residents – 'free euro' – from which funds could be transferred 1 : 1 into euro accounts abroad or non-resident euro accounts in the Netherlands. But the 'free euro' accounts could not be credited with direct transfers on a 1 : 1 basis from 'Dutch euro' accounts.

A spot exchange market would come into being where Dutch euros were traded against free euros and euros (both the same effectively). Dutch residents making payments to other euro-area countries to settle euro-denominated invoices would have to buy first freely transferable euros in the exchange market in exchange for their Dutch euros. The rate of exchange between Dutch euros and free euros would depend crucially on the policy intentions of the Dutch government. Given the hypothetical situation of exit from EMU occurring so as to escape deflation via devaluation, the Dutch euros would fall to a discount below free euros. And the authorities might indeed set a new parity with a permitted range of fluctuation (for example, 1.10 Dutch euros equal 1.00 free euros, with band limits of 1.13 and 1.07).

The Dutch banks would make an immediate exchange loss or gain depending on whether loans in euros to Dutch residents were more or less than deposits from Dutch residents. The package of measures accompanying exit from EMU would provide for a government compensation fund to cover extreme loss (defined as more than a stipulated percentage of bank capital). The package would also include orders regarding the denomination of debts outside the banking system. For example, interest and principal on government bonds would presumably be payable in Dutch euros. Debts due by Dutch residents to other Dutch residents could also be settled in Dutch euros. But euro-denominated debts and loans to non-residents, including euro-denominated bonds issued in international markets by Dutch residents, might remain payable in euros proper.

In practice the complexity of accounting work to be done to effect these changes would require some length of partial banking holiday and a temporary partial standstill on debt repayment to accompany the sudden exit from EMU. There may be no need to impose any suspension of clearing funds within the Netherlands. But payments in euros between the Netherlands and euro-area countries might have to be suspended for a period of days until the new accounting categories were in place and the exchange market between free euros and Dutch euros operational. On top of this, there would be the question of cash transactions. The only cash in existence would still be euro banknotes and coin, and these would be in effect free euros. The orders accompanying the exit from EMU would include one stipulating that euro cash could no longer be obtained on a 1 : 1 basis against Dutch euro deposits. Euro cash would trade 1 : 1 with free euros and at the same premium as free euros to Dutch euros. Dutch residents wishing to obtain euro cash against their Dutch euro deposits would have to effect an exchange transaction of Dutch euros into free euros. (In practice, euro banknotes could still be obtained from automatic teller machines, but the amount debited from the corresponding Dutch euro account would include a charge equivalent to the current premium.) The Dutch would not pay euro banknotes into Dutch euro accounts but into their new free euro accounts. (Banks would offer a facility whereby clients without a free euro account could still obtain the premium.)

In areas of the retail economy where payments are made in both cash and by card or cheque, dual pricing would apply. There would be a discount given for payment by euro cash – with the discount calculated from the exchange rate of Dutch euros against free euros. (For example, if 100 Dutch euros = 90 free euros, then a discount of around 10 per cent would be given for payment in euro notes or coin rather than by cheque or credit card where ultimate payment would be in Dutch euros.) Many retail prices in Dutch euros (for settlement by cheque or credit card) would not immediately rise following the suspension of EMU membership. Crucially most wage and non-wage costs would be paid in Dutch euros. The main exception would be a jump in the price for traded goods and services.

In the cash retail economy (where cash is virtually the only form of payment) most prices might through inertia remain unchanged at first meaning that they would rise in terms of Dutch euros. Competitive pressures, however, should subsequently bring some falls in cash prices (when expressed in terms of free euros or euro cash). The rise in purchasing power in the Netherlands of euro cash, both in the cash and (to a greater extent) non-cash economy would provide some reflationary impulse – additional to that coming from the devaluation of the Dutch euro against the free euro.

Eventually the Dutch central bank would start issuing its own notes (it would take several months at least to organize the printing process). The issue of notes would go along with redenomination. These steps would be taken only once full democratic approval had been obtained for the exit from EMU. If instead the democratic process had produced a verdict in favour of staying inside EMU, most probably a newly constituted government would have the task of organizing re-entry. That should not be difficult so long as there is 100 per cent confidence in the markets that the EMU debate in the Netherlands was now finally over and that there would be no new political initiative to bring about an exit. The Dutch government, in consultation with the ECB, the EU Commission, and euro-area governments, would agree on a re-entry date from which all the various types of euro accounts would be merged into freely transferable euros and all would be fully convertible on a 1:1 basis into euro banknotes. Dutch euro reserves at the central bank of the Netherlands would again become fully transferable on a 1:1 basis to other member central banks.

Suppose, instead, that the democratic process had indeed brought approval for making the forced exit 'permanent'. Then at the given date, say within a year of the emergency withdrawal, Dutch euro deposits and loans would be relabelled as florins on the basis of 1:1 translation, and the Dutch central bank would pay out florin banknotes on a 1:1 basis against Dutch euro (now florin) deposits with itself. (The organization and printing of the new banknotes takes some considerable time!) Debt obligations of Dutch residents repayable in Dutch euros (in line with already mentioned provisions where a broad distinction is made between resident and non-resident creditors) would be relabelled in florins. Wages and rents already payable in Dutch euros would now be redenominated in florins on a 1:1 basis.

Dutch households would dispose of their euro banknotes in exchange for florin notes at the going market exchange rate. These euro banknotes would tend to accumulate in the vaults of the remaining central banks in the euro-area who in turn would have found their deposits (from banks in their respective countries) increasing by a similar amount. The Dutch government would buy with euros the flotsam of euro banknotes, operating in accordance with an EMU separation agreement concluded between itself and the remaining members.

These purchases by the Dutch government would drain away the excess reserves created through the euro notes previously circulating in the Netherlands finding their way into other member central banks. (In principle, the Netherlands could abrogate all responsibility for redeeming its share of the total issuance of euro banknotes but that would bring about a crisis in the already likely strained relations between the Netherlands and its EU partners. And there would be no hope of transitional assistance from the ECB.) The Dutch government would issue bonds denominated in florins to finance its euro banknote purchases, and in turn the Dutch central bank would buy these against the florin banknotes which it was now issuing.

In sum, a quick exit for a small or medium-sized country from an EMU suffering from deflation is technically feasible. (The large country case is more difficult, as several if not all other countries might decide to leave simultaneously, and even if a shrunken EMU subsists, its nature might be substantially different from its large predecessor.) The same can be said for a small or medium-sized country exiting from an EMU where inflation has become rampant, with the aim of restoring price stability. Again, taking Holland as an example, the Dutch central bank would suspend the transferability of euro deposits (except for a small share backing non-resident deposits in the banking system) with itself to other EMU central banks.

Whilst the idea of an EMU exit was a subject of political debate, speculation might drive down interest rates (with respect to resident business) at Dutch banks to near zero or even to significantly sub-zero levels. The zero barrier could be broken if indeed it were widely believed that euro banknotes would become inconvertible on a 1:1 basis into Dutch euro deposits as soon as the possibly imminent exit were to occur and if the Dutch central bank were to start levying charges on reserve deposits held with itself during the period of political debate so as to discourage a massive increase in demand for these. Such charges would be inconsistent with present rules within EMU but nonetheless special dispensation might be given by the ECB Council in an emergency situation (see below).

The fall of interest rates would tend to exacerbate inflationary pressures in the Netherlands, possibly triggering an emergency break (from EMU) similar to in the previous illustration. An additional factor behind an emergency break would be a flight of borrowers from the Dutch banking system out of fear that loans would be revalued upwards. Dutch banks would not relend the money repaid (by the fleeing borrowers) to banks outside the Netherlands for fear of exchange loss were their country to quit EMU. Their piling up of liquidity at the Dutch central bank could result in severe liquidity crisis elsewhere in the euro-area.

Immediately following the break, euro banknotes would trade at a discount to the new Dutch euro deposits (subsequently to be relabelled florins) in line with an illustrative starting parity of say, 90 Dutch euros = 100 free euros (as set by the government), with bands of permitted fluctuation on either side. The windfall loss on their euro banknotes suffered by Dutch residents together with the climb of the Dutch euro against the euro would contribute to a fall in Dutch inflation. More important, over the medium term, in bringing down Dutch inflation would be the freedom now enjoyed by the Dutch central bank to follow a stricter stability policy than the ECB had done.

What are the disadvantages of the suddenly imposed EMU exit, as in the last two illustrations, compared to the phased withdrawal via the gradual introduction of a new national currency alongside the euro (at first on a 1 : 1 basis), as discussed in the earlier British pound illustration? First, there is the pre-exit speculative run-up or run-down of interest rates (with respect to resident business) in the national banking system together with possible liquidity or financial crisis (either in the country leaving when devaluation is expected or in the rest of the euro-area where revaluation is anticipated). It is far from clear how far the ECB could or would reduce such pressures by emergency lending to banks (either in the country under suspicion of leaving or in the rest of the euro-area, as the case may be). Second, the government may be forced by the prospect of a deepening financial crisis to effect an emergency exit from EMU even before democratic approval has been obtained. In principle, the exit could be reversed if the democratic decision goes against withdrawal, but the whole operation would impose significant economic costs. Third, redenomination into the new national money occurs initially to an arbitrary extent as ordered by the government, rather than on the initiative of the borrower or depositor. Fourth, there are the possible large translation losses in the banking system and the resulting burden on the national budget. Fifth, transaction costs would be high in the interim period when the only form of cash is euro banknotes which are not convertible on a 1 : 1 basis into the new money. Against these disadvantages, there are the advantages of, first, rapidity with which an exit from EMU can be made and second, the ease of effecting a substantial effective devaluation or revaluation of the new currency against the euro.

By contrast, if in the scenario of phased withdrawal (as in the illustrated case of the pound) there develop strong expectations about the new currency falling to a discount or rising to a premium against the euro the amount of speculative position-taking ahead of C-day might assume massive dimensions. (C-day is the start of Stage 2 when 1 : 1 convertibility between the new money and euros is suspended.) The chances of a systemic crisis erupting due to speculation or badly managed hedging by a major financial institution would surely be significant. What starts as a phased withdrawal might change into a sudden exit well before the end of Stage 1. The central bank would suspend 1:1 convertibility between the new national money and the euro, whilst simultaneously blocking transferability of euro deposits held with it to euro-area central banks. 'British euro' deposits, created by the emergency decrees that would accompany the sudden exit from EMU, and British pounds (already in existence from the start of Stage 1), would be fully convertible into each other on a 1:1 basis. The risk described of a phased withdrawal of EMU degenerating into a sudden exit could mean that interest rates on the currency under suspicion might already diverge to a large extent from euro rates even during Stage 1.

Exit induced by regional slump

The hypothetical case just described of a phased withdrawal accelerating into a sudden exit could well arise where the trigger to EMU exit is a prolonged slump in one country existing alongside inflation at the target level and at least moderate prosperity for the euro-area as a whole. For example, a huge real estate and construction spending boom might have burst in Spain and in its wake brought a severe economic downturn. In the context of EMU, Spain's road back to economic health could be long and hard. The price level in Spain would have to fall substantially relative to that elsewhere in the euro-area so that external demand would grow more rapidly and compensate for weak domestic demand. Recreating a national money, devaluing it against the euro, and slashing interest rates to very low levels, would promote a much faster economic rebound.

A mainstream political party in Spain taking up the case for EMU withdrawal might well not focus attention on the possible devaluation that would accompany the introduction of the new currency. Devaluations are often vote losers rather than gainers. Rather, the focus of attack might be ivory-tower central bankers in Frankfurt who have no concern for economic conditions in Spain – whether high inflation or high unemployment. And the given political party would surely find it a softer sell to persuade voters of the harmlessness of staged withdrawal rather than to frighten them with images of forced bank deposit and loan conversions, extended bank holidays during which they could not pull banknotes out of their bank accounts on a 1:1 basis, and a long period in which there would be dual pricing for most goods and services, according to whether payment was made in cash or by card. If indeed the political party advocating EMU withdrawal came into a position of power, it might face considerable difficulties in switching presentation totally and backing a sudden exit plan. Instead there would be a political bias towards phased withdrawal and keeping quiet about potential devaluation.

In the history of EMU to date (early 2004) the nearest example of a country falling into a depression where the rebirth of a national currency would have offered a fast route back to prosperity is Germany. That country joined EMU with a level of costs swollen by high wage inflation during the unification boom (1989–92) and by economically unjustified large wage-hikes in the ex-communist Eastern Länder. As the real estate construction boom turned into depression, the German economy was in need of low interest rates and a cheaper currency. In the second half of the 1990s that came about first, via a general rise of the dollar from mid-1995 until mid-1998 (against both the yen and European currencies) and second, during 1999–2000, via a fall of the euro against both the yen and US dollar. It was not obvious then that the German price level was too high relative to the French, given that France was emerging from the long period of economic weakness under the strong franc policy (1989–96).

Indeed, according to a short analysis by the Bundesbank (see its Monthly Report, August 2003), the Deutschmark was converted into euros (at the end of 1998) at a real effective exchange rate level against the currencies of other countries entering EMU close to the average of the years 1975–98. The point still not admitted (in the August 2003 article) was that on a forward-looking basis, the Deutschmark should have been converted into euros at a markedly cheap level by comparison with the average of the previous twenty-five years, when account was taken of the evaporation of investment opportunity in the German economy. There were several factors in that dwindling of investment opportunity, and these were not all absolutely evident in 1998 – albeit that there were some symptoms which could be picked up by perspicacious analysts. The symptoms included the vast overbuilding which had occurred in the five years following unification and which would weigh on the construction sector, and the squeezed profit margins in the manufacturing sector.

Indeed, according to the Bundesbank's own analysis, if unit labour costs in the manufacturing sector were used to assess the real effective exchange rate of the Deutschmark at the end of 1998 against other currencies entering EMU, then it was strikingly overvalued. But, unconvincingly, the Bundesbank dismisses that statistic, maintaining that the relevant comparison is for unit labour costs across the whole economy rather than just in the manufacturing sector. Yet Germany's comparative advantage in the global economy is as a manufacturer, and if exports were to compensate for weak domestic demand (particularly investment spending) then the manufacturing sector should have been super-competitive.

In subsequent years (2001–3) the particular problems of the German economy became more obvious. The world economic downturn of 2001 hit Germany hard, given that country's specialization in the production of capital goods. And the business-unfriendly policies of the Schröder government undermined the willingness of German companies to invest at home. The downturn in the construction sector accelerated. Meanwhile a general rebound of the euro against both the US dollar and Japanese yen added to the German economy's woes.

Under these circumstances (of the early 2000s) if the Deutschmark had still been in existence it would have floated down against the other European currencies (even though the history of the actual Deutschmark had been one of a continually appreciating currency within Europe). The Bundesbank would have driven interest rates down to near zero. Other European central banks would have followed to a considerable extent. Most probably there would have been no general fall of the dollar against European currencies in that situation. Under the regime of the euro, instead, the consensus of expert opinion in Germany swung to there being only one way out – deep structural reform, including the labour market and the social welfare system. EMU became an engine of turning back the social economic policies of the Schröder government. These policies may indeed have been feasible under the old Deutschmark regime. It would have made good economic sense if the Social Democrat Party led by one-time euro-sceptic Gerhard Schröder had started down the path of withdrawing from EMU.

In practice, such a move was unthinkable in the political climate of the early 2000s. How could his Social Democrat Party (SPD) explain to the electorate its complicity through the 1990s in the mistake (from the perspective of lost German prosperity) of the Maastricht Treaty? And there was still the unfinished business of integrating the East European countries in the EU that might have been jeopardized by a new coolness of Berlin towards EMU coupled with attacks on the policies of the ECB.

In principle, what programme for withdrawal from EMU could Berlin have submitted? An alluring approach for the German electorate could be the introduction of a new Deutschmark at a starting rate of 1:1

against the euro (the new currency would be distinct from the old Deutschmark that expired at the conversion rate of 1.96 DM/euro in 1999). There may have been no talk of devaluation – but of the need for a much more expansionary monetary policy to fight deflation. And, if successful, the end of deflationary depression in Germany should mean the reborn Deutschmark would be strong again. A policy paper from the government might have laid out the two main possible procedures for exiting from EMU – a staged withdrawal or an immediate exit. Given the seriousness of the economic situation, the preferred option would have been presumably sudden exit.

The special case of German threatened separation

Germany, however, in raising the possibility of an exit from EMU, would be in a very different situation from the UK (hypothetical), Spain, or the Netherlands. It is not clear that EMU without Germany would continue to exist. And, if it did, the exchange rate of the re-created Deutschmark to the much shrunken (in terms of geographical domain) euro would hardly be the central plank of German economic policy. Much more important, indeed, would be the conduct of monetary policy by the again independent Bundesbank. And inevitably, a German draft proposal of exiting EMU would bring policy responses from the ECB and from other euro-area countries aimed at salvaging the system. A German exit proposal would in practice include as a preliminary a bid for negotiations on reform of the present monetary order. What might German demands include?

First, there would be the question of ECB operating procedures. Berlin might press for a temporary (over several years) rise in the inflation target for the euro-area as a whole so as to facilitate a relative fall in German wages and prices. Second, German negotiators might demand that the ECB acknowledge that at some times German economic conditions should receive a greater weighting in policy-making decisions than simple economic arithmetic (Germany's share in euro-area GDP) would suggest (see p. 17). Third, Germany might request a larger say in ECB policy-making and propose, for example, that there be a chairperson of the policy-making council who is different from the ECB president, and who is by rotation the central bank governor of one of the three large countries (Germany, France and Italy). By rotation the ECB president should testify to the national parliaments of those same countries (rather than as at present just to the weak European Parliament). Fourth, if the present president of the ECB is viewed as incompetent,

Berlin might demand his early resignation (never mind the fixed eight-year term according to the Maastricht Treaty).

If the other euro-area governments – and in particular Paris – agreed to Germany's proposals it would surely be impractical for the ECB to put up any independent resistance. And, in any case, ECB board members would presumably be adverse to the loss of power for their institution entailed by a withdrawal of Germany from EMU. But suppose the EU governments failed to concede. And Berlin decided to carry out its threat of withdrawal. What form would the exit negotiations take?

A first point would be the willingness of the other members of EMU to remain in a monetary union without Germany. If all agree to persevere with monetary union, then the separation of Germany would be no different from the earlier examples above, except as regards size. The seigniorage agreement would be on a larger scale. The shrunken euro would be so much smaller that it might well suffer an important loss of international investment demand. The newly created Deutschmark might enjoy some immediate popularity as international investors reweighted the European section of their monetary and bond portfolios to include less euros (filling the gap with Deutschmarks). There would also be some shrinkage in international borrowing demand for euros. The exchange-rate path of the truncated euro against say the dollar would depend in part on whether international borrower demand shrank by more or less than investor demand. Also important would be perceptions of any weakening in the 'stability culture' of EMU without Germany as a member. A further factor would be the relative long-run investment outlook in the shrunken euro-area versus Germany. If indeed Germany were the sick man of Europe, then the euro would gain from the recreation of the Deutschmark.

The political anchoring of EMU without Germany would have to change, albeit that this could not take effect without some modification to present EU treaties. A euro-group of heads of state, a euro-group of finance ministers, and a euro-area caucus of European parliamentarians would take over responsibilities (the nomination of top officials at the ECB and the probing of its performance) from the present EU organs (EU Council of Ministers, EU finance ministers, and EU Parliament) – on the assumption that Germany remained a member of the EU. It would make no sense that Germany and the UK should have a major presence in decision-making bodies with respect to EMU when neither were members. The EU Commission might still provide expert services in the administration of the Stability Pact. But union countries might decide to create a Fiscal Policy Council, whose head would be appointed by the euro-group, for making tough recommendations (including ultimately the levying of fines) rather than leaving these to the EU Commission and EU Council.

The emergence of an independent Deutschmark might make all EU countries see advantage in the creation of a formal mechanism of monetary co-operation. Germany would set an inflation target in line with that of the ECB. The Bundesbank would invite an ECB board member to participate in its council meetings (not voting) and conversely. A reweighting of board members would take place at the ECB. With the German chair on the board now vacant, Spain and Holland might insist on permanent representation there. Indeed Holland would have some considerable negotiating power, as its decision to stick with EMU would be key to its final shape without Germany.

If Holland pulled out with Germany, then most probably so would Belgium. (The Dutch-speaking population in Belgium would oppose an affiliation to a French-dominated monetary union, seeing that as increasing the influence of the French-speaking population.) Luxembourg might remain in EMU – persuaded to do so perhaps by the offer to transfer the headquarters of the ECB there from Frankfurt. Austria might also remain in the union, attracted by the vision of its extension to include the central and East European countries and so the eventual recreation of a monetary union over most of the lands that once upon a time formed the Austro-Hungarian empire. France would be the largest member, followed closely by Italy, and, well behind, Spain. The small country members would include Luxembourg, Austria, and eventually the central and Eastern European countries. There is no clearcut basis for predicting how this severely truncated euro would perform in the world currency markets. The principles would be the same as for the previous example of how a less shrunken euro would behave. The exit of Holland and greater dominance by France might have some damaging influence on investor perceptions of the severely truncated euro.

If Italy opted to have its own currency again in the above situation, it would be impossible to salvage even a rump European Monetary Union. There would be no rationale for Spain, Luxembourg and East European countries joining effectively a French franc area. Germany's planned exit from EMU would bring about a dissolution of the whole. If the disastrous Austro-Hungarian precedent were followed then there would be a rush for the exit, with each country taking steps to introduce a new currency. Suppose Germany were the first out – effected by blocking transfers of euro deposits at the Bundesbank to other euro-area central banks and suspending German banks' obligation to convert resident euro deposits into euro banknotes or conversely on a 1 : 1 basis. Euro banknotes (and hence the euro) might fall in value versus the new German euro if investors took fright at their possible zero liquidation value when EMU finally ended (in the interim they would retain value as money in countries not yet out and as the only means of cash payment still in Germany until the new mark notes can be printed).

Total dissolution – and rebirth of the ECU

In practice, EU governments would surely agree a formula for dealing with euro banknotes prior to Germany's exit from EMU and the likely associated dissolution of the whole. A relaunch in revised form of the old EU basket currency, the ecu, which was converted into the euro at 1 : 1 at the start of EMU, would be an obvious solution. The new ecu basket would be composed only of the currencies issued by the members of the now defunct monetary union. (The old ecu basket contained all the various sovereign currencies of EU member states.) Each currency would receive a weight at the start that approximates the share of its issuing country in the total euro-area economy. The member countries would agree that euro banknotes should be convertible 1 : 1 into ecu deposits at any of their central banks. In turn national central banks in presenting euro banknotes to a central payments centre, perhaps the Bank for International Settlements (BIS) in Basel, would be able to obtain a portfolio of deposits (at the respective now independent national central banks) in the new national monies weighted as in the ecu.

The BIS would be in charge of settling payments for banknote redemption as due from the respective national central banks (as agents for their governments). Each government would issue bonds in their new national monies for the purpose of raising funds for the given redemption. Around the same total value of bonds would be bought by their central banks as the counterpart to their issue of banknotes in the new national monies. The governments would be able to reduce the old euro debt held by their central banks as the former received credits via the BIS in respect of their share of euro notes handed over for redemption. (Technically, the French government, for example, would present euro banknotes redeemed via the BIS to the Banque de France in repayment of euro-denominated government bonds held by the latter. The euro banknote liabilities and euro bond assets of the French central bank would fall in line.) In sum, dissolution as outlined would leave national seigniorage and government debt outstanding broadly unchanged.

In order to prevent ecu deposits ever rising in value significantly above their underlying basket definition, central banks would be obliged to create ecu deposits on request from any member bank in exchange for delivering a portfolio of the new national monies in the appropriate weights. The whole process of euro note redemption and new issue of national notes would take some considerable time. It would be at the initiative of individual citizens when to sell their euro banknotes for the new national banknotes once these became available. During an interim period euro banknotes would continue to be used but at a variable premium or discount to prices paid by cheque or card. The premium or discount would be determined by the exchange rate between the new national money and the ecu. Residents in any member country would obtain the new national notes when available by selling their euro notes converted first into ecu deposits for the national money in the foreign exchange markets. No doubt governments would make arrangements so that the exchange could be done at little or no cost to individuals (in effect giving a subsidy to the banks involved in the conversions).

All the banknote transactions described would take place only after the formal date agreed among the member governments on which monetary union was to come to an end. On the given date there would be an immediate cessation of intra-union transfers of central bank euro deposits and a mandatory conversion of resident deposits and loans into the new national monies (on a 1 : 1 basis). Euro banknotes and the new national money deposits would not be convertible into each other on a 1 : 1 basis. Non-resident deposits and loans would be converted on a 1 : 1 basis into ecus. Ecu deposits would be convertible on a 1 : 1 basis into euro banknotes and conversely. Spot exchange markets between the national monies and between the national monies and the ecu would come into existence from the given formal date. Forward exchange rates could be quoted from the date at which dissolution was decided upon (in advance of the formal date for dissolution).

In a country whose currency was expected to be weak, interest rates for terms stretching into the early post-dissolution period could reach fantastically high levels (on an annualized basis). Indeed, interest rates in that country might rise sharply even before any agreement on dissolution, driven by speculative expectations (and flight for safety). The country might be forced (by the imminent danger of a financial crisis) to withdraw from EMU prior to dissolution or even prior to any joint decision on dissolution, suspending the 1 : 1 convertibility of deposits into euros. The given country would agree, nonetheless, to follow the agreed procedures with respect to ultimate liquidation of euro banknotes and conversion of non-resident deposits and loans into ecus.

Ecu exchange rates (both spot and forward) would be constrained within very tight limits (set by transaction costs) by the possibility of converting the basket of underlying currencies into the ecu and conversely. Similarly, ecu interest rates would be derived by arbitrage with interest rates on the underlying currencies. Domestic government debt would be converted into the new national monies (except for bonds held by the central bank as backing to the outstanding issue of euro banknotes). Private non-bank debt would be converted (1:1) into the new national currency of the creditor and debtor if both were residents of the same member country. Otherwise conversion would be into ecus on a 1:1 basis. If investors or borrowers wanted to shift from ecu denomination to a new national currency, they could do so in the market by arranging swap and exchange transactions. As in the previous example (Germany withdrawing from EMU but the remains hold together), the EU governments might sign a monetary co-operation agreement which would bind themselves to mutual consultation over inflation and money supply targets, and mutual participation in new national monetary policy-making.

A complete dissolution of EMU is implausible except under the scenario of Germany deciding to pull out. A French exit would not in itself trigger wider pressures towards disintegration. All the remaining countries in EMU would most probably still see considerable advantage from remaining in the union. The difference is explained in large part by the smaller economic size of France and also by the structure of intra-European trade. There are a group of small countries whose trade is dominated by Germany but not by France. (See Chapter 1, p. 10, for a further discussion of this point.) Moreover, it is unclear what would be the catalyst behind a French withdrawal. France was the most persistent driver behind the process of monetary union.

Why would the French policy elite change its view about the geopolitical benefits of monetary union? The challenge to union if it ever came in France would surely come from a non-establishment source – perhaps some combination of the far right, Euro-sceptic Gaullists, non-mainstream socialists and communists. A Europe-wide deflationary depression would be the most plausible context in which EMU withdrawal could ever become a serious issue in French politics. And a bitter clash between Paris and its EMU partners over budgetary policy could help inflame anti-EU sentiment in France. Ultimately, a radical government in Paris might simply refuse to comply with budgetary admonitions from Brussels and implement an aggressive programme of public spending financed by borrowing. Its government debt market could fall into crisis, and a forced exit from EMU would become a possible scenario.

A withdrawal – whether forced or strategic – of Italy from EMU would similarly not trigger a general dissolution. In view of the long history of Italy's commitment to Europe and lack of any significant political opposition to the EU or to monetary union, it is highly improbable that a strategic exit would ever take place. Even if the unfavourable trends of recent years were to continue – with the Italian economy losing competitiveness through wages rising too fast relative to other EMU countries and the failure of a knowledge-based economy to grow and replace traditional manufacturing sectors under growing competitive pressure from developing countries – it is difficult to see the economic case for recreating a sovereign Italian money at a devalued rate against the euro gaining political support. Maybe a few disgruntled investors who regret the passing of the days of high interest income enjoyed before EMU and who have suffered large losses on alternative investments (for example, Argentian bonds, which were especially popular with Italian investors during 1999–2000) would vote for withdrawal. But in general the electorate would most likely see greater safety in the euro than a re-incarnated Italian national money given its dismal record for stability in is previous life.

The main possible scenario for an Italian withdrawal would be a forced exit, due to the political impossibility of tackling a widening of the budget deficit as the economy continued to flounder. The high starting-level of government debt to GDP in Italy is a point of vulnerability (in 2003 net government financial liabilities as a percentage of GDP amounted to 95 per cent in Italy versus 55 per cent in Germany). A flight from Italian government debt in a situation of political impasse to tackle a serious deterioration of public finances is not outside the realms of the possible. If in that situation the ECB stuck strictly to not bailing out the Italian government – even via providing loans to Italian banks in difficulties from holding large amounts of Italian government bonds – a forced exit from EMU could occur. (In Chapter 5, the no bail-out condition and how it might be strengthened as part of a reform of the Stability and Growth Pact are discussed.) The technicalities of how a forced exit would be organized are described below.

The danger of forced exits by Eastern European countries

Forced exits are most relevant in considering possible new members to EMU with fragile banking systems and governments of only middle-ranking credit status. Suppose, for example, that one of the Baltic countries makes it into EMU by 2008. A bubble develops in the economy which subsequently bursts. The banks find it hard to roll over foreign credits and domestic capital flight weakens their position further. The government budget balance moves into huge deficit (as tax revenue collapses in the declining economy). The warnings from Brussels over the continuing large breaches of the Stability Pact, gloomy reports from credit analysts and lack of feasible policy response cause bond prices in the given country to slump (as bankruptcy risks rise). The European Central Bank has already reached the limit of its lender of last resort function with respect to the country in question. The banks are faced with huge cash withdrawal demands from the distrusting public.

In that situation the country might have no alternative but to effect an emergency withdrawal from EMU. Deposits of euros at the Baltic central bank would become non-transferable to other euro-area central banks. The same deposits would no longer be convertible into euro banknotes on a 1:1 basis. Commercial banks would suspend simultaneously the 1:1 convertibility of deposits into notes. Euro banknotes would be quoted at a premium to Baltic euros, which would themselves trade at a discount to euros in the new spot exchange market. The central bank would make emergency loans to the banking system in 'Baltic euros' and make large-scale purchases in the market of Baltic euro government debt. It is not clear that a seigniorage agreement with the remaining members of EMU could be enforced or would be relevant. Most Baltic holders of euro banknotes might hoard them rather than sell them, albeit at a profit (paper), for the new currency. And even if some did find their way into the remaining European System of Central Banks (ESCB), the Baltic country would not be in a position to buy them back, unless granted official loans to do so.

Hence in admitting a less advanced economy into EMU the rest of the members take a risk of loss in the scenario of subsequent forced exit. The loss would be equal to the amount of circulating euros in the given country originally issued by its central bank but subsequently becoming the liability of the remaining euro-area countries. In effect, by not entering into any obligation to buy back its euro note circulation which seeps into the euro system, the government of the country exiting from EMU can derive much needed extra revenue in the form of seigniorage from issuing its own money. Banks would eventually be able to obtain Baltic euro banknotes – once these are printed – against their reserves at the Central Bank (by that point Baltic euros would have been redenominated). The government might delay, however, the final step of printing new notes and redenomination in the hope of arranging an international rescue package together with tough domestic austerity that would make possible a return to EMU.

The same conclusions apply to other extreme scenarios under which a forced exit from EMU would take place – for example if there were to be a war between Hungary and Slovakia, with Hungary already an EMU member, or between Poland and the Ukraine (with Poland already an EMU member). In these war-crisis scenarios the ECB would hardly provide assistance to the country in question to help stave off financial crisis in the given country. Rather withdrawal would become a self-fulfilling prophesy as interest rates rose sharply, debt markets collapsed, and banks neared default.

Existential and territorial risk are features of the euro

The various scenarios described in this chapter about how one or more countries can separate from EMU or how EMU might disintegrate completely have bearing both on market and political judgements about the euro. Though territorial and existential risks are not a totally new phenomenon in currency history, their previous appearance has been related to extreme political events – for example, the ceding of large amounts of territory by Germany after its defeat in World War I or the disintegration of the Austro-Hungarian empire. In the case of the euro, shrinkage of the euro-area via separation of one country (territorial risk) or dissolution (existential risk) could occur in far less than extreme political and economic circumstances.

We examine in Chapter 5 how investors should approach the topic of existential and territorial risk in their evaluation of the euro. In the short history of EMU to date, these risks have been regarded as trivial over any normal horizon relevant to investment appraisal. But were that assessment to change, then knowing investors would have to undertake a careful risk analysis. The existence by then of an agreement between EMU members as to some basic rules which would apply in separation or dissolution would help prevent the emergence of large risk premiums in the market against the dangers of the unknown.

It is understandable why such an agreement was not drafted before the start of EMU (for reasons discussed at the beginning of the present chapter). And even now, more than half a decade since the launch of the euro, an agreement would be controversial and difficult to achieve. Many members would view withdrawal as a beggar-your-neighbour policy – reducing the potential benefits from the creation of economic union and raising costs (transactions and exchange risk) for all. Unilateral solutions which could involve stealing large competitive advantage from the remaining members of the union should not be given any advance legitimacy. An unspoken fear could be that German power would be increased by any steps to make dissolution or separation easier or more respectable (in that a threatened German withdrawal could be a highly effective bargaining tool for the gaining of national advantage). The currency regime to be followed by Germany is a matter of high economic importance to all EU members and should not be redetermined at a national level.

The formal position is indeed that no country could change currency regime without the agreement of all (as required for a revision of the Maastricht Treaty). That is unrealistic. Forced exits from EMU might occur in the future due to a rise in the opinion polls of the backing for an anti-Maastricht party, despite 100 per cent politically correct behaviour by the government in office. An agreement on exit procedures, however, might not be achievable until the first forced exit has taken place.

Some opponents of European federalism might well sympathize with the view that an agreement on procedures for separation, and explicit recognition by treaty of the possibility that dissolution might occur, would be a good thing in itself. The Eurocrats at the ECB would have to take more heed of the opinions current amongst the various sovereign peoples. Monetary policy would be run by a process of political compromise or bargaining between the nations, with the background threat of dissolution or separation helping to forge decisions and narrow the potential gulf of alienation between the ECB and the various European citizens. The ECB would become firmly embedded in a confluence of national political streams rather than remaining an ivory tower.

Yet it is doubtful whether a continuously raised, albeit fluctuating, level of existential and territorial risk for the euro would indeed bring a consistent improvement in the economic conditions of the member countries. In particular, the euro money and bond markets would be segmented by varying risk premiums along country lines, and banking system risks could be substantial. The best working mode for EMU would be a normally zero level of territorial and existential risks. There are obvious merits in reforms to the ECB's structure that would help to reduce those risks by reducing the gulf between the present ivory tower and the European peoples (see Chapter 5 for reform proposals). Even so, the throw of the economic and political dice could make separation or dissolution eventually inevitable. The implicit strategy of the EMU founders to suppress disintegration by creating the legal fiction of permanence for their promised union will almost certainly prove to be flawed.

4
Journey to Permanent Union

A paradox in the process of monetary union is that it started with President de Gaulle sending Raymond Barre to Brussels in summer 1967 (as a vice-president of the European Commission). De Gaulle was an opponent of European federalism. He viewed with suspicion all granting of power to European supranational institutions, of which the not-yet-conceived European Central Bank would have been a prime example. He was in favour of European integration that took the form of direct intergovernmental co-operation in which the Bonn–Paris axis would call the shots. Such had been the design of the so-called Fouchet Plan (aimed at co-operation in foreign policy and defence matters) that the general had backed without success at the start of the 1960s (having become president of France in 1958).

De Gaulle might one day have approved a model of European Monetary Union if it were constructed between a small number of sovereign monetary authorities firmly embedded in national political systems, with fully spelt-out exit possibilities. There would have had to be no doubt about Paris and Bonn (later Berlin) being in control of policy-making. What was to emerge thirty years later was very different – a federal European central bank, with the French and German central bank presidents having only one vote each – the same as for every other member country, in a policy-making council of eighteen persons, including six permanent board members with no national office. And there was no visible exit. Yes, Germany's monetary power had been destroyed. But in the process the most powerful of all European bureaucracies (the European Central Bank) had been created and France had gained no influence. The lead architect of the first blueprint put out by Brussels on monetary union was none other than Raymond Barre, albeit that this did not spell out in any detail the full extent of federalism which was to characterize the final construction.

From the Barre Plan to the Paris Summit, 1968–72

According to one of Barre's biographers, Henri Amoureux (1994), de Gaulle's instructions to Barre had been blunt: 'I attach a great importance to Brussels. I only want to send there young and dynamic people. I have not done all that I have done to see the European Community turned into simply a free-trade area once England gets through the door.' That was not an instruction to prepare a grand plan for monetary federalism in Europe. In a press conference in early 1964 de Gaulle had stressed that power and executive responsibility should belong to governments and not to 'international experts [in Brussels] who tried to succeed where Caesar, Charlemagne, Napoleon and Hitler had failed'.

Barre remained faithful to de Gaulle's anti-'Anglo-Saxon' instincts – preparing detailed papers in 1971–2 as to why sterling's reserve role made it impossible for the UK to join the European Community – but not to de Gaulle's hostility to supranationalism. Already, in February 1968, Barre had proposed a monetary plan of action (narrowing bands of permitted fluctuation for Community currencies against each other, mutual consent to parity changes, and a common unit of account). That was quite tame. During the next year much more effort went into the design, and Barre in February 1969 published a comprehensive plan for monetary union.

Barre had impressed de Gaulle the previous November (1968), advising him strongly to stand firm and reject a devaluation of the French franc – defying intense pressure from Bonn. Having earned the general's considerable respect, Barre could win him round to the idea that his monetary plan would indeed bring back influence for France on the European monetary stage lost during the autumn 1968 crisis. Barre's opposition to devaluation had not been a cynical political manoeuvre but based on a strong view that exchange-rate change could bring no lasting economic benefit – a view that had indeed stimulated his interest in monetary union and was to colour his later role as a co-founder of the European Monetary System (1978).

The Barre Plan of February 1969 had yet to be adopted as Community policy. That happened at the Hague summit of Community heads of state in December 1969. The general had resigned in April (1969), and the new President Georges Pompidou had based his election strategy on making inroads into the centre-ground of French politics. There the idea of Europe was popular, particularly amongst the Catholic Centre. And so Pompidou had promised a widening (to include the UK) and deepening of the European community (closer integration).

German support for a deepening via monetary union was still uncertain. The Grand Coalition government in Bonn (formed in autumn 1966) included CDU politicians who had opposed Adenauer's attachment to a German-French alliance and were suspicious of any initiative that could weaken the crucial ties between Germany and the USA. (Indeed, Adenauer had not succeeded in gaining parliamentary support for the French-German Friendship Treaty signed with de Gaulle in 1963 without making major concessions to the opposition within his own party. These had the effect of diluting the treaty substantially.) Ludwig Erhardt, whose liberal reform programme in 1948 had been widely credited as a catalyst to the ensuing seventeen-year German economic miracle, had been as economics minister under Konrad Adenauer (1949–63) and subsequently chancellor (1963–6) a staunch opponent of all talk of monetary union and a committed Atlanticist (including a strong advocate of UK entry into the EU). His influence was still considerable on opinion within the CDU and more widely.

In autumn 1969, however, a Social Democrat-led government had come into power in West Germany. The new Chancellor, Willy Brandt, was committed to a path of détente with the Soviet Union and its east European satellites, and recognized that closer political and economic integration in Western Europe would help allay fears of Germany 'going its own way'. Also a big realignment of the French franc against the Deutschmark had now taken place – the first since 1961 – with the new French government devaluing its currency in the summer (1969) and the new German government revaluing in the autumn. German industrial lobbies were voicing concern about the loss of competitiveness suffered. The time was ripe for an initiative to enhance currency stability in Western Europe especially as the Bretton Woods international monetary order based on the US dollar looked increasingly fragile.

The Hague Summit (December 1969) adopted the aim of European Monetary Union to be achieved over a ten-year period and set up a committee (in which experts delegated by the member countries worked alongside Raymond Barre at the Commission) under the chairmanship of the Luxembourg prime minister, Pierre Werner, to prepare a report. The Werner report was published in October 1970 and accepted by the Council of Ministers in March 1971. The report contains several key concepts that were later to be picked up by the Delors committee (1988). Monetary union was to proceed in three stages – with the first characterized by co-operation and a narrowing of the ranges within which member currencies could fluctuate against each other. In a second stage, left vague, there was to be progress in achieving convergence between the European economies. In the final stage the Community was to form 'a single currency area within the international system, characterized by the total and irreversible convertibility of currencies, the elimination of margins of fluctuation of exchange rates, the irrevocable locking of parities and including a Community organization of central banks'.

It was implicit that the latter organization would pursue the centralized monetary policy required. There was also considerable discussion in the report about the need to co-ordinate and set limits on national budgetary policies. But key issues, on which there was considerable disagreement amongst the member states, were left unanswered. What would be the nature of the common monetary policy? In particular, what would be the policy on inflation? That question was in turn intimately related with exchange rate policy. For as long as the European countries pegged their currency to the US dollar they would tend to import US inflation. This had been aggravated by the Vietnam War and was about to be driven much higher by the new Federal Reserve chairman (from early 1970), Arthur Burns, as he injected massive monetary stimulus to the US economy in support of President Nixon's re-election strategy.

Ultimately, would there be a co-ordinated unpegging of Community currencies from the US dollar so as to insulate the European Community from US inflation shock? What would be the relationship of the new organization (of central banks) to governments? Would it be firmly under the control of an EU ministerial stability council dominated by France and Germany or would it be an independent federal-style institution, similar to the Bundesbank? The report alluded to economic policy, including budgetary, being determined at a community level, but how would this be consistent with French resistance, in particular, to abdicating national sovereignty in these areas? And the passage towards monetary union, involving the transfer of powers from national to community bodies would surely require amendments to the Treaty of Rome?

In mapping the journey towards monetary union, the Werner report reflected an uneasy compromise between two main views of how European monetary integration should proceed. On the one hand there was the monetarist position (nothing to do with Milton Friedman!) spearheaded by Raymond Barre. According to this, freezing the exchange rates between the member currencies would itself be instrumental to bringing about the underlying economic convergence which would be essential to the success of monetary union. Indeed the extreme monetarist position (not put forward by anyone on the Werner committee), would be that monetary union could be introduced almost immediately as it would bring about the needed convergence by force of shock. (That would still beg the issues as to the nature of the common monetary policy and political responsibility.) On the other hand there was the 'realist' position, to which German and Dutch negotiators in particular adhered to, that there had to be considerable progress in economic convergence (inflation, growth, labour market and social structures, removal of barriers to capital flows) before a serious start could be made on monetary integration.

The compromise was that in Stage 1 there would be a narrowing of bands for exchange rate fluctuation between European currencies – in the hope (not high amongst the realists) that this would help along the process of economic convergence and ultimate monetary union. In practice, however, the compromise was not implemented because in early May 1971 Germany set the Deutschmark free to float, responding to a massive inflow of capital inflows driven by the aggressive US monetary expansion being pursued by the Arthur Burns Federal Reserve. Bonn proposed to its EC partners a joint float of European currencies against the dollar, but Paris was opposed. A joint float would mean accepting the hegemony of the Deutschmark – better to stay with the dollar, press for reform of the international monetary system, and wait for Germany to re-enter. And that is what happened – or seemed to have happened – when a new global fixed-exchange rate system was ushered in by the Smithsonian Accord (December 1971).

In April 1972, the Community countries implemented the Basel Accord (technically an intergovernmental rather than EEC agreement), creating the 'Snake in the Tunnel' whereby the exchange rate fluctuations between their currencies would be held within much narrower margins than those which would be derived from the bands against the dollar as in the Smithsonian Agreement. At a summit in Paris in October (1972) the original six members and the three new entrants (UK, Denmark and Ireland joined formally in January 1973) declared that economic and monetary union was an objective of the community. (That declaration was later quoted at Prime Minister Thatcher to break her potential but never exercised veto on new progress towards monetary union in the late 1980s.) When in February and March 1973 the Smithsonian system broke apart, the EC countries (with the exception of the UK which had dropped out of the Snake in summer 1972) continued to keep their currencies in the Snake.

French monetary failure derails the EMU train, 1974–83

Barre's monetarist position was soon to be put to a test. Would exchange rate stability between the franc and mark force France and Germany to follow convergent monetary policies (and adopt similar anti-inflation aims) in the face of the inflationary storms which now raged? The answer was not long in coming. In January 1974 France pulled out of the Snake, having failed to follow Germany in taking vigorous monetary action to quell the inflation fire. In July 1975 France re-entered the Snake, amazingly at the same parity as before, despite much higher inflation than Germany in the interval (January 1974 to July 1975), and unsurprisingly had to re-exit in March 1976.

The second exit by France in little more than two years did not mark the end of the 'monetarist' approach to European Monetary Union. Two years later (March 1978), at a bilateral summit in Aix-La-Chappelle, President Giscard d'Estaing and Chancellor Helmut Schmidt resolved to push ahead with new plans for exchange rate stabilization, having as their ultimate aim progress towards monetary union. The French prime minister was then Raymond Barre, chosen by Giscard d'Estaing as successor to Jacques Chirac, who had resigned in summer 1976 (setting up his neo-Gaullist party). Barre doubtless reckoned that the monetarist approach was still valid if combined with sound economic policy, which had unfortunately not been practised by his predecessor (Chirac). Soon after his appointment as prime minister, Barre introduced his plan for stabilizing the French economy. The plan consisted of structural reforms including the liberalizing of industrial prices (removing price controls). Though described as a monetarist with reference to monetary union, Prime Minister Barre had no belief in radical monetary cures when it came to reducing inflation. He expected that deregulation and a return to budgetary orthodoxy would gradually do the trick.

Helmut Schmidt, himself an economist, had no confidence in the monetarist approach to monetary union. But he had high respect for Raymond Barre and reckoned that the new French prime minister (who was also at first his own finance minister) could deliver the degree of economic convergence – particularly as regards inflation – that would allow the European Monetary System to work well. Moreover, Schmidt and Barre both saw US monetary policy as the villain which lay behind the sharp swings in the Deutschmark versus other European currencies, especially the French franc. When the dollar was under attack, as through 1977–8, international funds flew into the Deutschmark, pushing it higher against the French franc, Italian lira and British pound, and crippling thereby the German export sector. The EMS, if successful, would limit these swings in intra-European exchange rates and so reduce exposure of the German economy to US monetary shocks. And, as explained in Chapter 1, Schmidt saw closer monetary co-operation in Europe and the controlling of 'Deutschmark nationalism' as desirable as part of a longer-term strategic vision for the Federal Republic. In any case, the Bundesbank ensured that the final form of the European Monetary System was not very different from the old Snake, and not thereby a serious challenge to German monetary independence. The main distinction was that the new system was anchored in an EC framework, and that a new common monetary unit of account, the ecu, was introduced.

The European Monetary System came into existence finally in early 1979 (following a short delay during which Paris held out for a concession in the Common Agricultural Policy). Prudently – at least it appeared so to Prime Minister Barre – the French franc entered the EMS at a parity that was highly competitive for the French economy (the franc had fallen steeply between its exit in mid-1976 from the Snake and the start of the new system). But there was a contradiction here. If the franc appeared safe from any major devaluation for a considerable time ahead, then it would be impossible for French interest rates to rise

7   Giscard and Schmidt know how to play music
Source: Reymond, *Tribune de Genève*, June 1978.

significantly above German rates (otherwise there would be perverse huge money flows into France). Yet with inflation in France at 8–9 per cent p.a. compared to 3 per cent p.a. in Germany, a severe monetary squeeze – similar to what Volcker was soon to introduce in the USA – would be essential to bringing about quick convergence on inflation between the French and German economies. The monetarist approach to European monetary integration (fix exchange rates first) was in direct conflict with the realists (foster convergence, particularly of inflation, before seriously proceeding towards monetary union). According to the realists, a severe monetary squeeze in France and a bringing down of inflation there to the German level was a first step in the integration process.

Eventually, if the new fixed parity between the franc and mark had been adhered to, anti-inflationary forces in France would gradually have built up. As French inflation continued to run faster than German, the traded goods and services sector in France would have come under increasing competitive pressure. A downturn there would have gradually spread to the whole economy – and weakening demand would have brought a decline in French inflation. But this disinflationary mechanism failed to become operational in the actual circumstances of the late 1970s due to the sudden surge of the US dollar (related to the aggressive tightening of monetary policy by the Federal Reserve under Paul Volcker which saw short-term US rates rise to 20 per cent p.a.). As global funds turned to the US dollar, the Deutschmark was particularly weak, meaning that France had no scope to introduce a monetary squeeze unless seeking first a temporary revaluation of the franc within the EMS. In any case, the political calendar would not have allowed Barre to introduce a powerful anti-inflationary policy at this time given the approach of presidential elections (May 1981), at which President Giscard d'Estaing would face a severe challenge not just from Mitterrand at the head of a socialist–communist alliance but also from Chirac and his neo-Gaullist party.

The counter-factual historian can speculate what would have happened if Giscard (rather than Mitterrand) and Barre had won the spring 1981 elections. The overall strong dollar and the counterpart of a weak Deutschmark (induced in addition by the new threat from Soviet nuclear missile deployment in Central and Eastern Europe) through the early 1980s may well have allowed Barre to persevere with an unchanged parity for the franc against the mark right through until 1985 – at the cost of growing misery in that part of the economy competing with Germany (but not with the US and other dollar zone currencies). The crisis (for Barre's monetarist approach) would have come with the collapse of the dollar from spring 1985 onwards. Could Barre really have kept his head in the sand and counted on balance being restored in the French economy by prices and wages in the non-traded goods and services sector falling sufficiently so that businesses in the traded goods and services sector could regain international competitiveness and profitability? All other experience in the world suggests that once the inflation battle had been won via a growing overvaluation of the national currency (the French franc in this case) bearing down on the export sector, there would have to be a devaluation by a substantial margin. An essential flaw in the monetarist approach to monetary union was to deny the likelihood of that final parity change.

There were in fact two possible roads to bringing French inflation down to German from the perspectives of the late 1970s. The Volcker road was almighty monetary squeeze accompanied most probably by currency appreciation (and possible pegging for a transitory period at a highly overvalued rate), followed by monetary relaxation and depreciation once the mission was accomplished. The Barre road was easy at first via stabilizing the currency at an unambitious level, but hard-going after a possibly long delay, with the export sector suffering the rising burden of its front line position in the struggle against inflation. That suffering of the export sector would probably go on for longer than under the short-lived currency appreciation which accompanied the start of Volcker road. If the Barre road eventually reached its destination of stability, the currency would have to be devalued in order to halt an onward journey into deflationary depression.

Re-starting the journey, 1984–8

It was not evident that the Barre road would lead any earlier than the Volcker road to a point at which the next serious steps could be taken towards monetary integration in Europe. Indeed, even if the Barre road were pursued to its end without switch in direction, the time taken to overcome inflation would most probably be considerably longer than for the Volcker road. Does this mean that Barre and the birth of the European Monetary System in 1978 were obstacles in the way of monetary integration?

That would be too harsh a judgement on Barre. His biggest contribution to the cause of monetary union was to put a long-term plan on the agenda (in 1969) that facilitated and promoted its formal adoption as an aim of the European Community. But it is plausible to argue that monetary union could have been reached by the same date (1999), if not sooner, had the European Monetary System never been launched. Indeed the final decisive run-up to monetary union in the years 1993–8 occurred against the background of the EMS having been virtually disbanded (with the margins of permitted fluctuation for bilateral exchange rates widened to 15 per cent either side of parity).

Did the existence of the European Monetary System facilitate Mitterrand's strategy switch in March 1983 away from socialism to Europe? Superficially yes. Jacques Delors, then the French finance minister, used the opportunity of an emergency meeting of the EC Monetary Committee in the midst of the latest crisis of the French franc (mid-March 1983) to create a spectacle. In this Delors could display apparently tough negotiating skills, once deployed to great effect as a Christian trade union official. He demanded a sizeable revaluation (upwards) of the Deutschmark to accompany the inevitable further devaluation of the French franc, or else France would pull out of the Exchange Rate Mechanism (ERM). The threat was not awesome. Yes, a pull-out might have brought a steep initial fall of the French franc – greater than under a managed devaluation – but the fall would surely be reversed once the French government inevitably proceeded to tighten monetary policy further. Furthermore, given that the Dutch guilder would move with the Deutschmark, and the Italian lira together with the Belgian franc would not lag far behind, a Deutschmark revaluation was virtually the same as a devaluation of the French franc. The demands of Delors in fact amounted to little more than that Germany participate in a face-saving operation for Paris.

The Kohl government, flush from its first election victory two weeks earlier, acquiesced, but 'demanded' in return that France should finally put its house in order (meaning a reinforcing of anti-inflationary policy and budget austerity). That demand would doubtless favourably impress the industrial lobbies in Germany, which would resent a new competitive advantage being awarded to France. And it is what Delors wanted to hear. He returned to Paris from Brussels and, with the backing of Mitterrand, proceeded to effect the U-turn away from socialism in France. There was no other way, Delors could assure his French TV viewers. The choice was between preserving the European Monetary System (which only France had threatened to leave!) and accepting the reasonable conditions imposed by its partners there, albeit at the cost meanwhile of sounding a retreat on the road to socialism in France, or heading towards national bankruptcy outside Europe. At a deeper level, however, the European Monetary System was the well-chosen stage-set for the U-turn, rather than an essential element in the defeat of high inflation and new progress towards European monetary integration.

During the first two years of the Mitterrand administration the franc had been virtually floating – albeit with large step moves in line with three devaluations rather than continuously. The scare of socialism and the capital flight which it provoked meant that a severe monetary squeeze could indeed be imposed in France during the early 1980s without the corollary of an overvalued currency and an export sector bleeding profusely (as happened in the USA and UK). France was pursuing the Volcker road to low inflation but without the normal accompaniment of a jump in its currency. But the squeeze on the non-traded goods and services sector of the economy had to be correspondingly greater (as there was no disinflationary influence coming to bear via the export sector).

There is little reason to doubt that France, just as every other major OECD country, would have succeeded in lowering its inflation rate by the mid to late 1980s, irrespective of whether there had been an unchanged Deutschmark parity for the franc within the context of the European Monetary System between March 1983 and April 1986 (when Finance Minister Balladur in the newly elected centre-right government under Prime Minister Chirac effected a further devaluation). And with an inflation rate down to the German level by the mid-1980s, the stage would have been set with or without the European Monetary System in existence for serious negotiations between France and Germany on progress towards the Community aim of monetary union.

Of course, 'setting the stage' for serious negotiations depended on much more than French and German rates having converged, even if that was an essential condition. The personality mix was important. It can be doubted whether a Schmidt–Mitterrand or Kohl–Giscard or even continuing Schmidt–Giscard partnership could have steered Europe through the key preparatory stages for monetary union. Schmidt had low regard for Mitterrand's unreformed socialism (even if the sincerity of the French president's commitment to the programme was in doubt) or understanding of economics. Giscard had deeply offended Kohl by divulging his pre-election confidences to Schmidt. And in any case Giscard was perhaps incapable of making the conciliatory gestures that mattered so much in the deepening of the Kohl–Mitterrand relationship (Giscard wept tears in a television broadcast over Mitterrand's decision to invite the German army to participate in Bastille Day celebrations, and when Berlin was still divided he had insisted on a presidential visit on treating the Western part as distinct from the Federal Republic).

Helmut Kohl had become chancellor in November 1982, after the small centre party, the FDP, had deserted the coalition government led by Helmut Schmidt (Social Democrat party) and joined a coalition with the Christian Democrats (CDU).

The first half of 1984 brought key developments in French–German co-operation to drive European integration forward. France held the presidency of the EU and Mitterrand used the opportunities to its full of 're-launching Europe under a French flag'. At the EC Fontainebleau Summit (June 1984), UK Prime Minister Thatcher was cornered into accepting the final offer on an EU budget rebate and in return unblocked progress on other matters. Kohl and Mitterrand agreed to Jacques Delors as the next president of the EC Commission (from January 1985) even though by rotation the job should have gone to a German. Mitterrand invited Kohl to make the important symbolic gesture of jointly attending a memorial service at the Verdun battlefield that same October.

Jacques Delors wasted no time in moving ahead with his new mission. He identified the creation of a single unified market for goods and services as the theme which would unite and provide a springboard for the ultimate aim of monetary union (now central to Mitterrand's European strategy, albeit not yet promoted publicly). Significantly Delors appointed himself as Commissioner for Monetary Affairs (a post he held in addition to the presidency). Astutely he chose Lord Cockfield, who Prime Minister Thatcher respected, as the Commissioner in charge of pushing forward the Single Market programme (dubbed 'Europe 1992' or 'Europe without frontiers'). As early as June 1985, the decision was taken, at the Milan EC Summit, to launch an intergovernmental conference for the purpose of drawing up a new treaty required for the implementation of the Single Market. (The necessary authority did not exist under the Treaty of Rome originally setting up the European Community.)

Delors realized that abolition of restrictions on capital flows were seen by London as a fundamental step towards the creation of a Single Market. The Bundesbank and the German finance ministry were in favour of such reform. And so, alongside the drive to the Single Market, the new Commission president drafted directives for the full liberalization of capital movements (programme agreed in July 1986).

Delors and Cockfield did not produce from scratch the massive tomes of required national legislation to create a Single Market. Much of the material had already been produced under the previous Commission. But Delors drove the process forward decisively and joined it to a restatement of the old aim of monetary union in the Single European Act (the new EC treaty required to implement the unified market).

Delors argued that the liberalization of capital flows and the development of a Single Market would require ultimately monetary integration. National monetary policies could no longer be pursued effectively in a Europe without any exchange restrictions and continuing exchange rate uncertainty together with occasional sharp currency moves would prevent the economic benefits emerging of a Single Market. The main opposition to Delors on restating monetary union as an aim came from UK Prime Minister Thatcher. But at the Luxembourg European Council Meeting (December 1985), the UK conceded some ground.

First, the old objective of monetary union as agreed by the Paris Summit of October 1972 was to be restated in the preamble to the Single Market Treaty. Second, article 102A, carefully crafted by Hans Tietmeyer (then 'sherpa' of Chancellor Kohl on international economic issues), incorporated a monetary dimension as demanded by Paris and Delors (mentioning benefits of further monetary co-operation), but made clear that any new institutions could be established only on the basis of a new treaty. The Single Market Treaty was eventually signed at the Hague in February 1986 and came into force a year later.

The build-up of momentum in the process of monetary integration following the Single Market Treaty took even Commission President Delors by surprise. The bursting of the bubble in the US dollar (which reached its peak in spring 1985) was one factor. With the collapse in the US currency the Deutschmark again came under upward pressure against the French franc as international funds sought refuge in the world's number two currency. The new strains within the European Monetary System culminated in a revaluation of the Deutschmark in spring 1987, just one year after the realignment of spring 1986 initiated by Balladur, the French finance minister (immediately following the victory for the centre-right in the parliamentary elections). The forced second devaluation of the franc was resented by Balladur, then active in the international forum of G7 putting together the so-called Louvre Accord (under which the USA, Japan, and Europe in February 1987 committed themselves to stabilizing the dollar after its steep fall since the Plaza Accord of autumn 1995).

Even so, it was a surprise development when Balladur started to talk in late 1987 of the benefits of a European Central Bank. The French finance minister's new stance on that issue was surely at odds with the coalition agreement between the UDF parties (centre-right) and neo-Gaullists, signed in spring 1986 at the start of the new government under Prime Minister Chirac. This had ruled out new steps being taken towards European monetary union. Cynical commentators could suggest that Balladur's warming in winter 1987/8 towards the idea of a European Central Bank was driven by the election strategy of his Gaullist party boss, Jacques Chirac. Presidential elections were due in spring 1988 and Chirac was particularly fearful of the looming challenge there in the first round from Raymond Barre whose power base was the pro-European centre-right (see Madelin, 1998). (In the second round either Barre or Chirac would face Mitterrand.) More generally, the entrenched pro-Europe sentiment in the Catholic centre of French politics – the key battleground between Gaullists and Socialists – was crucial to the progress towards European monetary union. Balladur, in any case, was not envisaging a single European currency but closer monetary co-operation and an increased role for the ECU as common currency (see Chapter 2). He circulated proposals to other EC finance ministers for moving on to a next step. President Mitterrand, in uneasy 'cohabitation' with the Conservative government, took advantage of this new stance of its finance minister to himself promote the cause of monetary union.

Also in late 1987 German Foreign Minister Genscher threw his weight behind a new drive towards monetary union. His position in Chancellor Kohl's coalition government had been strengthened by the considerable progress of his Free Democrat party in the Bundestag elections of that autumn. And keenly aware of the new opportunities for Germany in relations with the Soviet Union under President Gorbachev he saw the advantage – as did Willy Brandt almost twenty years earlier – of calming French and other West European fears by offering to intensify Germany's integration into the European Community. It took some time, however, for Chancellor Kohl to be convinced of the case for backing a new initiative towards driving forward monetary union. There were some headwinds.

In January 1988 when Kohl had come to Paris to commemorate the twenty-fifth anniversary of the Élysée Treaty, agreement had been reached on setting up a French-German economic council (regular meetings between French and German senior economics officials, including central bankers and finance ministers). But the Bundesbank had dragged its feet, insisting that its political independence be in no way compromised. Chancellor Kohl had to be sure that the Bundesbank would go along in public with his next pro-EMU move, and his inclination was still that this should take place only once the Single Market was complete (1992).

Behind the scenes, however, Jacques Delors was working on the chancellor – taking advantage of the German presidency of the EU during the first half of 1988 to pull all the strings. Thus in March 1988, Chancellor Kohl made a pro-EMU speech (albeit cautioning that a European Central Bank was 'perhaps not for tomorrow'), and Stoltenberg, the German finance minister, pronounced himself in favour of moving forward. Crucially Bundesbank President Pöhl, in a speech around the same time (March), spoke favourably about the eventual creation of a European Central Bank. He insisted, however, that first all EC countries should join the exchange rate mechanism (ERM) and second, the new money must be as reliable as the Deutschmark. It is probable that Hans Tietmeyer, on whom Kohl lent heavily for advice concerning international economic policy questions, was still lukewarm at best towards a new initiative (there is no direct evidence on this point). By early June 1988, however, the die was cast, and a favourable decision towards moving forward had been taken in the German chancellery. In France, Mitterrand had gained a second seven-year term in the May presidential elections, and in the subsequent parliamentary elections his Socialist party had regained power.

Delors and Pöhl compose the blueprint, 1988–9

At the Hannover EU Summit of late June 1988, the decision was taken to set up a committee under the chairmanship of Jacques Delors to draw up a blueprint for European Monetary Union. The Committee was to consist mainly of the central bank governors from each of the EC countries with a few outside experts (including Lamfalussy, then General Manager of the Bank for International Settlements). Mitterrand had not wanted finance ministers to be included. His own finance minister, Bérégovoy, was no enthusiast of monetary union. Moreover, finance ministers would be reluctant to relinquish budgetary powers and control of their central banks – both key conditions of the monetary union about to be designed. Genscher had wanted a committee of experts. Thatcher had opted for central bankers, believing they would be very cautious. Delors had accepted the eventual compromise, confident that he could use the authority of a virtual central bankers committee to produce a report of considerable political weight.

The committee was dominated by Delors and Pöhl, whose relationship was not without friction. It is hardly surprising that out of the committee as composed no new brilliant ideas emerged. The dusted-down Werner report, produced seventeen years earlier, was the starting-point. The old stumbling blocks could now be neatly sidestepped. There was no need any more to consider an 'economic government' and how to reconcile conflicting national objectives in monetary policy. All were agreed that the European Central Bank should have one and only target – price level stability. No one around the table (mainly in Basel after the regular monthly meetings of the G10 central bankers at the BIS) believed that there was any role for activist monetary policy. Once popular ideas, whether about a trade-off between inflation and unemployment or the scope for monetarily fine-tuning the economic cycle, that had stymied the Werner Committee (in that member countries would have different preferences regarding the ideal combination of unemployment and inflation or the appropriate amount of fine-tuning) were regarded as obsolete by the present drafters.

What better way to eliminate possible national political conflict behind the scenes in the European Central Bank than adopting the Bundesbank model whereby all central bankers would be strictly independent of their governments. What central banker would not support that? And when it came to automatic rules to limit the scope of national fiscal independence which central banker would not embrace strict limits on budget deficits? And they could do so in good conscience, if indeed that troubled them, given the prevailing popular view that Keynesian economics was bankrupt and that budgetary policy should be pursued in strict conformity with long-term stability rules.

One could say that the Delors report emerged from the abyss of almost twenty years of failed macro-economic management and popular revulsion against inflation: forget about actively steering the economy and hand over the keys to a group of independent central bankers in an ivory tower, whose geographic location was still to be determined. It is doubtful whether that conclusion would have found consensus support even from a central bankers' committee fifteen years later (2003), after the experience of three huge economic bubbles and their subsequent bursting (Japan 1987–93, Germany 1988–95, USA 1997–2003) and of the deflationary dangers which came in their wake. Abandoning monetary or fiscal policy activism at both the national and European level would surely have looked a perilous step. But accepting the case for activism would mean an infinitely more complex blueprint for monetary union – if indeed it proved possible to put one together. In 1988, however, central bankers were kings. They had successfully battled the hated inflation and they promised a new age of prosperity under their simple stability framework. The old hoary question of whether monetary union could proceed without political union could now be conveniently by-passed. Power to the central bankers and the fiscal policy watchdogs in Brussels!

The journey to the promised land of prosperity under a Europe-wide stability framework was to be made by stages, and here the Delors committee unsurprisingly displayed no suppleness. In the first stage, to start in July 1990, there was to be closer monetary co-operation, new surveillance by Brussels of the EC economies, and a complete freedom of capital flows (exchange restrictions to be totally scrapped). In the second stage (starting date unspecified) candidate countries for the monetary union had to prepare themselves. They would have to adopt statutes of independence for their central banks (if not already independent) and rein in budget deficits into compliance with set limits. At some undetermined point in Stage 2, a European Monetary Institute (not yet formally named as such) would be created. This would not be responsible for present monetary policy but for constructing the framework in which the European Central Bank would operate eventually. The Monetary Institute would be the forerunner of the European Central Bank.

There was some difference of opinion in the committee as to what specific roles the European Monetary Institute would have during Stage 2 but this could be left for intergovernmental negotiations in preparing the new European Treaty (without which the legal authority for proceeding would not exist). Stage 3 (full monetary union and the launch of the European Central Bank) could not start until a quorum of countries had satisfied the four eligibility criteria: first, a high degree of price stability; second, sustainability of the government financial position; third, the observance of the normal fluctuation margins provided for by the European Monetary System and no devaluation within the last two years; and fourth, durability of economic convergence as illustrated by long-term interest rates.

The third eligibility criterion – good behaviour in the EMS – was the most troublesome at both a theoretical and practical level. After all, the 'monetarists' on the Werner committee had surely by now lost the argument to the 'economists' (mainly in the German and Dutch delegations), who had argued that economic convergence should come before the fixing of exchange rates. In particular, French experience in the 1970s and early 1980s had dramatically illustrated the failure of exchange rate fixes on their own to bring convergence. Why could not the EU countries proceed to monetary union without the straight jacket of premature fixing of exchange rates?

Indeed, if the economies were converging, intra-European exchange rates should become more stable in any case, and so why superimpose the 'no devaluation in the previous two years' criterion? Yes, there may have been good theoretical grounds for the extent of exchange rate variability over the previous few years to be used as a market test of whether underlying convergence had yet occurred. But such a test to be meaningful would be best performed where considerable flexibility in intra-European exchange rates were possible and no greater weight would be given to downward than upward fluctuations of any currency. It would be the standard deviation that mattered most.

It would have been totally unrealistic for any member of the Delors committee to propose scrapping the exchange rate mechanism of the EMS on the way to European Monetary Union. (The ERM was the system of bilateral parities, ecu par values and intervention bands that constrained the fluctuations of exchange rates between member currencies.) According to the consensus view, the ERM was an essential building-block in the process of monetary integration. But could a consensus have emerged that the continuation of a flexible EMS (with frequent parity changes) should not in itself be a barrier to progress towards the goal? After all, the final exchange rate at which any particular currency merged into the new European money could have been left to late-stage negotiations between governments and the Commission rather than depending on the freezing of arbitrary parities for two years. The critical negotiation would have been between France and Germany on the relative entry rates for their two currencies.

There is no evidence that the Delors committee ever deliberated along these lines. Delors himself as French finance minister (1981–4) had made no further devaluation against the mark into the central plank of macro-economic policy in spring 1983. Why would he go along with a proposal that seemed to provide a new opportunity for French go-it-alone socialism or, in the future, go-it-alone radical policies by a Gaullist government? And Germany had long seen the principal practical advantage of the European Monetary System as the ruling-out of competitive devaluations by its main trading partners, most of all France. The asymmetries of the EMS had allowed Germany to have some benefits of exchange rate stability within Europe without itself sacrificing monetary independence (so long as the Deutschmark remained the anchor currency in the system).

From a German standpoint, it was a risky enough enterprise to eventually renounce the Deutschmark in favour of a new European currency. Why meanwhile add to the woes of the German export sector by seemingly permitting France to gain new competitive advantage? Indeed, if the carrot of monetary union could prevent the competitive devaluations of the early years of the Mitterrand administration (1981–3) from recurring, all the better. And there was a practical point. If monetary union depended on the French and German governments agreeing on an entry exchange rate between their two currencies, it might never happen. Expedience demanded that the exchange rate be imposed arbitrarily by history – specifically the parity of around French franc/Deutschmark 3.40 agreed at the EMU crisis meeting of spring 1987.

The premature locking of the crucial exchange rate between the franc and the mark encouraged by the Delors committee's design of eligibility criteria for monetary union proved to be an economic disaster for both France and Germany in succession. The approaching shock of German unification should have brought an initial sharp appreciation of the mark and subsequently an even bigger depreciation. Instead, the quasi-fixed rate between the franc and mark pushed France and later Germany to the brink of deflationary depression. But that is running ahead of the story – and certainly no member of the Delors committee had any greater prescience than the general pubic about the momentous events about to occur in Central and Eastern Europe. These would power the train forward to monetary union at a speed that no one inside or outside the Delors committee could have expected.

Indeed, the Madrid EU Summit (June 1989) brought a temporary stalling. In the cool language of the final communiqué necessitated by the need to compromise with the opposition of Prime Minister Thatcher, 'the European Council considered that the report … fulfilled the mandate given in Hannover'. Chancellor Kohl, facing adverse opinion polls at home, was disposed towards foot-dragging (abandoning the Deutschmark could become a vote loser). The Bundesbank was only too glad to go along with this. The formula for delay was that the next major step – the opening of an intergovernmental conference to design the new treaty essential to implementing the Delors proposals – would take place after the start of Stage 1 (July 1990), and before then there would be 'full and adequate preparation'. No dates had yet been set for the start of the second or third stage and there were many details yet to be filled in.

Chance would have it that France occupied the presidency of the EC in the second half of 1989. And at the September meeting of finance ministers in Antibes, a high-level working group was set up under one of Mitterrand's inner circle, Elizabeth Guigou, with the purpose of drawing up the list of topics to be considered by the intergovernmental conference. That should be full and adequate preparation enough! But would Chancellor Kohl see it that way? His attention by now was focused on 'the German question'. Over the summer months there had been the growing exodus of East Germans via the newly opened frontier between Hungary and Austria into West Germany. Then on Thursday 9 November 1989 the Berlin Wall opened.

German reunification and the leap from Strasbourg to Rome, 1989–90

In seizing the historic opportunity to realize German unification, Chancellor Kohl in the subsequent few months took two huge monetary gambles. The first was a headlong monetary union with the East, which he viewed as essential to winning votes for his Christian Democrat Party in the first and last free elections to be held in the German Democratic Republic (DDR). (See the related discussion on this point in Chapter 2.) Second, Kohl released the brake on progress towards European Monetary Union, encouraged to do so by France's backing (albeit not instantaneous) of German unification and by Brussels agreeing to immediate EC entry for East Germany (an astute move by Jacques Delors!). In addition, Kohl was convinced that a new step towards integrating Germany into Western European should calm fears that his unified nation intended to throw its weight around. These fears had been provoked in part by Kohl's refusal at first to clearly state that a United Germany would accept the Oder-Neisse frontier with Poland as permanent. Already at the Strasbourg EU Summit (early December 1989) – where there had been considerable distrust of Kohl's dash for German reunification – Germany agreed that the intergovernmental conference on EMU (the new treaty) should start by the end of 1990. But many sceptical commentators interpreted 'should start' as far short of absolute commitment to a given deadline.

In a walk along the beach near Biarritz in early January 1990, Kohl and Mitterrand overcame the brief cooling of their relationship in the previous December (when the French president had made visits to President Gorbachev to discuss the German question and to the dying communist regime in the DDR). In April 1990, Kohl and Mitterrand addressed a letter to other EU heads of state calling for two parallel intergovernmental conferences, one to discuss a treaty on monetary union, the other political union. In the Dublin Summit of June 1990, the EC Council resolved that both conferences should start that December. At a Rome Summit in October 1990, the EU council agreed (with the UK dissenting) that the second stage of the monetary union process should start in January 1994, and that a new monetary institution, subsequently named the European Monetary Institute, should be created at the start (of Stage 2). A firm date was fixed for the start of the two intergovernmental conferences (14 December 1990). Chancellor Kohl had finally dispelled the doubts publicly aired by Delors, amongst others, that autumn (1990) about whether Germany really desired monetary union. (In September 1990, Bundesbank President Pöhl had made public a letter sent to Kohl advising him to delay any agreement on the start of Stage 2 until there was greater economic convergence in Europe.)

The serious setback (at Rome) for Prime Minister Thatcher's strategy on European Monetary Union contributed to her downfall a few weeks later. She had neither succeeded in braking the journey towards EMU nor making sure that the UK would be a co-driver of the train. Yes, in the last resort, the UK could have exercised its veto, even at this late point in Rome. The momentum towards monetary union had now reached such a level that the countries keen on proceeding to union would most probably have attempted to proceed by way of intergovernmental treaty outside the EU framework. That would certainly have delayed the journey, possibly fatally. But Prime Minister Thatcher lacked the necessary support from within her divided cabinet to pursue such a bold, if dangerous, course. The follow-on from Rome in the politics of Thatcher's Conservative party was to ignite a civil war between the Europhiles, who charged that the UK had been left out in the cold, and the Eurosceptics, who saw her inability to stop the EMU train as due to treachery within the cabinet.

EMU builders continue work despite German economic hurricane, 1991–3

Just as the political momentum towards EMU had built up during late 1989 and 1990 to push the process decisively forward, and the UK brake had finally failed, the economic case for delay or at least some rerouting of the journey had become stronger than ever before. But Delors, Kohl, and Mitterrand were setting the pace impervious to, or uninfluenced by, contrary economic argument. One is reminded of the famous cartoon by Jaques Faizant at the time of the 1963 French-German friendship treaty, depicting General de Gaulle and Chancellor Adenauer with the caption (de Gaulle speaking) 'Hurry up, Konrad, you are not eternal'. This time, the hurry to beat the political and human clock was to have much more serious economic consequences.

German reunification, especially in the way it was taking place, was likely to bring about considerable divergence in the performance of German and other European economies. There was no way in the autumn of 1990 of predicting confidently the extent or duration of the divergence. In that situation it was foolhardy to take steps that would limit the flexibility of exchange rate change between the Deutschmark and other EC currencies. If, for political reasons, monetary union were to be pressed forward nonetheless, then there was a strong case for at least building in greater scope for exchange rate adjustment during Stage 1 and Stage 2 than had been envisaged in the Delors report.

At one extreme, United Germany could experience a long economic miracle as huge investment opportunity in the East and rapid productivity gains there stoked the engines of growth (also in the West). In this scenario, the real external value of the Deutschmark would rise and remain high over a long period as Germany swung towards being a long-term importer of capital. True, premature and botched monetary union between East and West Germany had already diminished the probability of miracle by autumn 1990, but the possibility still existed and was within the mainstream of probabilistic vision. At another extreme, reunification could impose huge burdens on the old West German economy as East Germany became a Mezzogiorno (the depressed Southern Italian economy). In that case the long-term equilibrium real value of the mark would fall.

As regards the short- and medium-term equilibrium path of the mark, much would depend on the skill of Bundesbank policy. If the central bankers in Frankfurt were to underestimate the inflationary pressures from German reunification (given the way in which it happened) then the mark might at first fall. It would subsequently rise sharply once a monetary squeeze was imposed. When monetary policy eventually switched back to an easy stance, the mark would fall. Whether it reached a trough well above or well below its real external value on the eve of German reunification would depend on whether there indeed had been an economic miracle or not.

If, despite the great potential swings in the mark's equilibrium real external value, the train to EMU proceeded along a route where the exchange rate between the French franc and Deutschmark rate in particular were frozen in nominal terms, what would be the economic costs? Their distribution (between countries) and their severity would vary along the course of the journey. For illustrative purposes we concentrate here on France and Germany. If the Bundesbank were to initially underestimate inflationary pressures arising in Germany from reunification then a stable mark (in nominal terms against the French franc) would go along with a real appreciation versus the franc. France would enjoy some external stimulus (both from strong German demand and some real depreciation of its own currencies versus the mark). This would be offset in some degree by the dampening effect on French domestic demand of the rise in French interest rates in line with German.

Once the Bundesbank switched from unintended accommodation to monetary squeeze the French economy would have to bear the double blow of higher interest rates (French rates rising at least in line with German) and the prospect of weaker German demand. Moreover, the French traded goods and services sector would reap less and less additional advantage in the form of rising German costs as German inflation decelerated. In sum, the French economy would become subject to powerful deflationary forces.

When eventually the Bundesbank relaxed its squeeze, sharp interest rate cuts would occur in France and Germany, and economic recovery would get under way in both countries. But the French economy might already have sunk into critical condition (with a degree of slack much greater than in Germany). Further ahead, however, there might be a reversal of fortune as the German economy were weighed down by the high level of wages left behind by the inflation excesses of the unification boom and a by a collapse in the construction sector due to speculative overbuilding. Indeed, a hangover of excess capacity from the boom-time might afflict a wide span of industrial sectors. Then Germany could risk falling into deflationary depression.

How much better the economic outcome for France and Germany might be if exchange rate flexibility and some degree of monetary independence were maintained, albeit at the political cost of slowing the speed of the EMU train towards its final destination! (How much worse if markets were to lose confidence in the French government's currency policy and hence the French economy were to be burdened by crippling high interest rates during the depressionary post-unification period!) Under a flexible exchange rate regime, the franc would fall against the mark during the period of German monetary squeeze and French monetary conditions would be consistent with low inflation and domestic economic equilibrium. There would be no depression, deflationary or otherwise in the French economy. When the German monetary squeeze were relaxed, then the franc would begin to recover somewhat. In the final stage, marked by German economic underperformance, it would be German interest rates that would fall well below French, with the Deutschmark depreciating against the French franc. The German economy would be spared a prolonged recession and the dangers of a deflationary depression.

The illustrative scenario depicted above of how an inflexible franc–mark rate followed by premature monetary union could impose severe costs on first the French and then the German economies is of course quite similar to what has actually occurred in the one-and-a-half decades following unification. The designers of EMU back in 1990–1 can be excused for not having perfect foresight. But they are guilty of not having at least considered the possibility that a rush to monetary union and a rigid defence of existing exchange rate parities in the immediate aftermath of German unification could produce seriously harmful economic consequences. The actual conditions encountered along the route were well within the sights of skilled scenario-builders and did indeed appear in several contemporary forward-looking market and economic commentaries.

Of course the apologists for the EMU designers can say that a fixed nominal exchange rate for the franc against the mark was not an essential component of Stage 1 or the early part of Stage 2. There could have been frequent realignments of the franc–mark parity along the way. In principle the mark could have been revalued in the second half of 1991, when the Bundesbank started to impose a monetary squeeze, and France could then have cut its own interest rates sharply. The revaluation would have been presented as temporary, with a strong hint as to a subsequent reversal (speculation on a future appreciation of the French franc would have allowed interest rates in France to fall far below German levels). Later, when the German economy eventually started to slow sharply and eventually underperform the French, the Deutschmark could have been devalued.

But such a flexible co-ordination of parity changes along the way to EMU was far removed from the mindset of the main policy-makers. There is some hint from reported statements that Bundesbank President Pöhl favoured a mark revaluation in 1990 and early 1991. But there is no evidence that he envisaged a subsequent devaluation. The mark had never been devalued before (against other currencies in the ERM) and the Bundesbank was firmly committed to a hard currency doctrine. The prejudice of economics officials in Bonn, including Hans Tietmeyer, was most likely in favour of mark stability (in real terms) within Europe rather than endangering long-term competitiveness of German industry.

In France, from spring 1988 to spring 1993, Pierre Bérégovoy as finance minister and subsequently prime minister (from spring 1992) was adamantly behind a strong franc policy (no devaluation against the mark). Egged on by his two senior economic officials, Trichet and Hanoun, Bérégovoy viewed a franc devaluation as certain to spoil the recently achieved near price level stability in France. The two officials argued that any scope (provided by devaluation) to reduce money market interest rates would be only temporary and that long-term rates, more important than short in business decision-making, might even rise perversely (on concern about higher inflation in the long run being induced by currency depreciation).

Bérégovoy would not have been won over by the further argument that a franc devaluation, even if temporary, might cause a slowing of the train towards EMU (in that there had to be two years of no devaluation prior to any country joining). He lacked enthusiasm for the project as designed (see Chapter 2). But Trichet and the Élysée Palace certainly took the danger of triggering a delay in the journey towards EMU seriously. The advocate of a franc devaluation in 1991–2 could well have argued that this would be the last and so it should present no impediment to monetary union by the end of the decade. But a devaluation then could have led on to further knock-on turbulence. Officials in conventional mould were most concerned about the possibility of a vicious circle of higher French inflation (set off by the initial devaluation) and further downward adjustment of the franc. The real concern should have been that there might have to be a subsequent devaluation of the Deutschmark in the second half of the 1990s. That could delay the journey, given the requirement of two years of no devaluation first. The way round that constraint would have been for there to be a long Stage 2, running from say 1994 to 2004 (or to no fixed date but whenever a core group of countries was ready to move forward).

But Mitterrand, Delors and Kohl were all in a hurry. There was a trade-off between the economic benefits of stretching out Stage 2 and the risks of the political winds in Europe turning against monetary union. At the Maastricht Summit of December 1991, Mitterrand persuaded Kohl to accept early deadlines for the start of Stage 3 (full monetary union) – 1997 if a majority of countries had by then satisfied the entry requirements, and 1999 for any countries (however few) eligible. If the 1999 deadline were not met then there was no obligation in the treaty for union to go ahead at a later date. This added to the time pressure.

Mitterrand knew that it would not be him that would be taking France into EMU. His presidential term would end in spring 1995, and in spring 1993 parliamentary elections were due at which opinion polls already suggested that his Socialist party would suffer a landslide defeat. In June 1992 he called a referendum in France to approve the Maastricht Treaty. The referendum was not necessary by law but Mitterrand could see clear political advantage in holding one.

First, the coalition of centre-right parties was deeply divided over the issue (the Gaullist party split 50-50, whilst the centrists were almost entirely in favour of the Treaty) and a referendum could weaken their united front in the run-up to the parliamentary elections. Second, if Maastricht were approved by popular plebiscite it would be more difficult for a future French government of whatever colour to pull out of the integration process.

The plebiscite took place on 20 September 1992 in the immediate aftermath of a major crisis in the European Monetary System which had resulted in a devaluation of the Italian lira and the withdrawal of the British pound. The wafer-thin majority for Maastricht did not prevent a huge wave of speculative capital outflow hitting the franc in subsequent weeks.

The trigger behind the new speculative storm was the ever tighter monetary squeeze being imposed by the Bundesbank under its new president, Helmut Schlesinger (who had succeeded Pöhl in August 1991 for a fixed period of two years). French domestic economic conditions called for much easier monetary policy, not tighter, and speculation was rife that Paris and Bonn would agree on a realignment of the franc–mark parity which would allow this to happen. In principle, as we have seen, such a skilfully presented realignment (hinting at a future reversal) could have been designed and without the EMU train coming to a halt, even if it had been forced to slow down for a while.

Markets were in no doubt about the opposition of the French government under Prime Minister Bérégovoy to a change in the franc–mark parity. The Élysée Palace was committed to the cause of monetary union, and there was little prospect of Germany trying to soften the French resistance. By late 1992 there was growing evidence that Germany was slipping into recession. The big industrial lobbies there would not welcome a new setback from a French devaluation. Chancellor Kohl faced difficult new parliamentary elections in less than two years. True, a devaluation of the French franc and sharp fall in French interest rates might have meant that German rates would rise by less or start their decline sooner. In consequence the Deutschmark might have been less strong than otherwise against the dollar. But all of that was uncertain, and there was no advocate to make the case. The basis of speculation against the franc in autumn 1992 was that the Socialist government's days were numbered. Parliamentary elections were due in spring 1993 at which the centre-right and neo-Gaullist parties were expected to win a landslide victory. And was France's Byzantine president to be trusted totally?

The autumn 1992 crisis of the French franc came and went after massive intervention and bizarre monetary tightening in the midst of low inflation and recession by the Banque de France (still under the command of the Finance Ministry). But in summer 1993 the day of reckoning finally came. Markets suspected that the new centre-right government in Paris under Prime Minister Balladur was less strongly committed to the 'strong franc' than its predecessor. These suspicions were strengthened when Jacques Chirac, the power behind the scenes as head of the Gaullist party, appeared to criticize Balladur for being too cautious in monetary and exchange rate policy.

The downward pressure on the franc became irresistible and at the end of July 1993 an emergency meeting took place in Brussels between EC finance ministers and central bankers to discuss the next moves. French requests for an emergency easing of German monetary policy fell on deaf ears. The eventual outcome was what looked like the effective end of the exchange rate mechanism (ERM) in the European Monetary System. Bands of permitted fluctuation were widened to 15 per cent either side of unchanged parities, compared to the previous 2.25 per cent. A chorus of Euro-sceptic commentators celebrated the apparent major setback or even fatal blow to European Monetary Union. And Jacques Delors himself briefly countenanced the failure of his main project.

Tietmeyer oversees damage repair after EMS storm, 1993–4

The reality was, however, that monetary union had never depended on France pursuing an economically suicidal interpretation of stability between the franc and the mark. And the steep recession now gripping Germany meant that the upward potential of a virtually freely floating mark against the franc was quite modest. It might not be long before the Bundesbank started to ease monetary policy, possibly as soon as late summer, when Hans Tietmeyer would succeed Schlesinger as head of the Bundesbank. (In fact, Schlesinger himself would almost certainly have eased policy aggressively over the next year as a whole.) Moreover, the legal requirement for a member's currency to have remained within its ERM bands and without any devaluation for two years prior to being admitted to union could still be satisfied. All these points dawned gradually on market opinion over the late summer of 1993. In addition there was the surprise that the Banque de France, now free from the exchange rate restraint, did not move swiftly to ease monetary policy sharply. Contemporary evidence suggests that Hans Tietmeyer and Claude Trichet played key roles in forestalling such a move – Tietmeyer calling the shots and Trichet smothering any enthusiasm in Paris for exercising the newly acquired monetary freedom (now that the old constraint of narrow ERM bands had burst apart).

Bernard Connolly (then a senior official in the EC monetary department) testifies that Tietmeyer gave a heavy-handed warning at the Brussels crisis meeting at the end of July against any rush by France and other EMS partners to exploit the new super-wide bands in the ERM and ease monetary policy (see Connolly, 1998). Implicitly his concern was that a run-up of the mark against the French franc would hit German export industry hard at an already very bad time (Germany was also in recession during 1993). It would be better (from a German economic standpoint) for French and German monetary policy to ease in step from later in the year onwards once German inflation was definitely subdued.

What would happen if France ignored Tietmeyer's wishes? The implicit threat was that Tietmeyer, about to take over the reins at the Bundesbank, and an arch Kohl loyalist, could throw spanners in the way of progress towards EMU, a cause for which he had never shown any individual enthusiasm but rather dutiful co-operation (with the chancellor). Trichet rapidly got the message through to Prime Minister Balladur, who already had ambitions of being a presidential candidate in 1995 and realized that support of the solidly pro-Maastricht centre vote would be essential to success. Trichet himself was en route to becoming governor of the Banque de France, newly independent of the government from the start of 1994, where he could make sure on his own that Tietmeyer's wishes were complied with.

What would have happened if Prime Minister Balladur had defied the Tietmeyer–Trichet axis, insisted on a substantial easing of French monetary policy in late summer 1993, and installed an independent-minded candidate (less truculent than Trichet to Tietmeyer) as first governor of the newly independent Banque de France? It is possible that Tietmeyer's bluff would have been called. The Bundesbank would have accelerated and sharpened its subsequent easing of policy in response to the franc's fall against the mark and the new disinflationary pressure which that brought to bear on the German economy. The French franc might have temporarily hit a low of say 3.75 francs/mark rather than 3.55 francs/mark but it could have been safely back to 3.45 francs/mark by 1997 as the French economy entered a strong economic recovery. And the depression-induced deterioration in French public finances which was one of the biggest potential obstacles to the EMU train moving forward in the mid-1990s might never have been.

In the climate of summer and autumn 1993, however, Balladur was not inclined to take a gamble in economic and European policies. Yes, Kohl might force a slighted Tietmeyer to still toe the EMU line. But the shock of the exchange rate mechanism (ERM) almost falling apart and the show of power by Germany at the Brussels crisis meeting (where, as we have seen in Chapter 2, Tietmeyer abrasively confronted the French negotiators, including Trichet) had impressed on Paris that the Kohl–Mitterrand relationship in itself was no guarantee of the EMU train reaching its destination.

Perhaps not too much notice had to be taken of the familiar rumbling by German Finance Minister Waigel, who in August 1993 declared that it was unimportant whether monetary union took place in 1999 or 2003. But the message from European central bankers also was that potential obstacles lay ahead. In July, Wim Duisenberg, then Head of the EC central bankers committee, had publicly said that it was difficult but not impossible for EMU to start on time. He meant what he said, for that autumn (1993) he turned down a request from Hans Tietmeyer to present himself as a candidate for Head of the European Monetary Institute (EMI) which was to be launched on 1 January 1994 (at the start of Stage 2). (He accepted a second request three years later – see below.) Tietmeyer took the occasion of the annual Federal Reserve research conference at Jackson Hole (late August) to repeat publicly his view that big gains by the Deutschmark were not desirable. At an EU Summit in October French negotiators revealed the weakness of their position (in the aftermath of the summer 1993 crisis) by conceding that the EMI – and thereby the European Central Bank – would be in Frankfurt. Lamfalussy was to be the stop-gap first president, with a fixed retirement date in late 1996.

A ruling by the German Constitutional Court in October 1993 that Germany could indeed join EMU so long as the new currency would be as strong as the Deutschmark allowed Stage 2 to start on time (1 January 1994). And, indeed, during the next year (1994) the prospects for monetary union on schedule (1999) improved, not least because of a strong economic recovery throughout the European Community. The German political calendar was the main cloud on the horizon – with Chancellor Kohl facing a difficult challenge in the Bundestag elections (autumn). In spring 1994 it was still unclear whether Oskar Lafontaine, a leading SPD contender, might make EMU an issue in the campaign (eventually he decided against). And Kohl faced criticism within his own party. (The financial support for Kohl's campaign from French coffers has already been discussed under the heading of the so-called 'Leuna affair' in Chapter 2.) In November, EMI President Lamfalussy floated for the first time a proposal for delaying the introduction of banknotes in the new currency until January 2002 (three years after the start of Stage 3). A warning of how far Germany had lost competitiveness during the unification boom and reinforcing Bundesbank opposition to any significant fall in the French franc was news in late 1994 that Mercedes had decided to build a new factory in Lorraine (Eastern France) rather than Bavaria (home state of Finance Minister Waigel).

Following the election victory of Chancellor Kohl in late 1994 the focus of political uncertainty became France, where presidential elections were due in spring 1995. Chirac was viewed with some suspicion by EMU-enthusiasts, given his past inconsistency on Europe and his reputation for opportunism. And indeed during the election campaign he had spoken of a referendum before finally renouncing the French franc. In reality, Balladur was most probably a bigger risk for EMU occurring on schedule if at all. If Balladur had become president it is most unlikely that he would have embarked on the severe budgetary tightening undertaken by Jacques Chirac and his firmly pro-EMU Prime Minister Juppé in very difficult circumstances. Balladur was a gradualist and never a convinced supporter of the single currency – and at a personal level did not 'hit it off' as well as Chirac did with Kohl.

Pressure grows to slow the journey, 1995

By the time of Chirac's triumph (May 1995) the economic skies were again darkening and the stalling of European economic recovery was an important source of the budgetary deterioration, most of all in France but also in Germany, that was to pose the next major obstacle to the EMU train. The source of the economic setback included the brief cyclical slowdown in the USA (following a severe tightening of Federal Reserve policy through 1994 and then the Mexico shock in early 1995) and a new sharp decline in the US dollar (related in part to the Clinton administration's economic conflict with Tokyo). During summer and autumn 1995 there was understandably considerable doubt in financial markets as to whether the new administration in France would see through the severe budget cutbacks necessary to achieve the yardsticks set in the Maastricht Treaty for eligibility to join monetary union (budget deficit to be less than 3 per cent of GDP). In the currency markets, the franc fell to almost 5 per cent below its old floor to the Deutschmark (before the August 1993 widening of bands). That move reflected a dominant, if questionable, view in the currency markets that a long delay in achieving EMU, or its abandonment, would bring a strong rise of the Deutschmark against the French franc.

The evidence available suggests that it was not a foregone conclusion that the Chirac administration would push through the highly unpopular cutbacks essential to meeting the Maastricht timetable for monetary union. (In the election campaign Chirac had promised 700,000 new jobs by the end of 1996!) First the new president had to be convinced that Germany was seriously committed (to the timetable). During summer 1995 there were accumulating signs of second thoughts on the other side of the Rhine. Finance Minister Waigel was leaking proposals that the budgetary rules under EMU would have to be specified in greater rigour than that so far applied in the text of the Maastricht Treaty. In September the German press speculated that Waigel was seeking to delay the start of EMU by one to three years under the slogan of 'stability before deadlines'. Bundesbank President Tietmeyer declared that the timetable should take second place to proper foundations. Doubtless all these negative comments were influenced in part by what was happening on the ground – a surge of capital flight into Switzerland on the part of small German savers frightened by the prospect of monetary union.

Their fears had been stoked by the collapse of the Italian lira in early 1995 as speculation on an Italian state bankruptcy went wild (contagion from the Mexico crisis?). How could the German saver trust the currency of a European Monetary Union that most likely would include Italy? Indeed the lira's fall and the 'unfair' advantage this gave to Italian competitors of German and French industry increased in some respects the likelihood that Italy would eventually be brought into the union. The mood amongst industrialists in Bavaria, for example, was that leaving Italy outside the union, free to pursue competitive devaluation, would undermine the main purpose of promoting a single market in Europe for goods and services.

Amongst the few voices expressing optimism on the train to EMU continuing on schedule was Bundesbank Chief Economist Otmar Issing, who in mid-September (1995) expressed the view that 'the point of no return had already been passed'. This confidence in the euro-project may have been one favourable point counting towards his later nomination to the most powerful position in the ECB board (behind the Dutch chairmanship). But it was not a confidence shared by Jacques

Chirac. In October he sought and obtained assurance in a summit meeting with Kohl that Germany was 100 per cent committed to the Maastricht timetable. The delay in securing that front before moving forward on budgetary policy was explained in part by Chirac's insistence on a series of nuclear tests in the South Pacific which enraged much of German public opinion and froze for several months further scope for French–German diplomacy on Europe.

Chirac accepts German terms, the train re-starts, autumn 1995 to mid-1996

In principle President Chirac could have presented a multi-faceted proposal to Chancellor Kohl. Yes, the French government will move ahead with severe budget cutbacks essential to meeting the Maastricht timetable. But you (Chancellor Kohl) must assure us that all the noise coming out of your country about delay is noise only. You will also have to understand that there must be an accompanying substantial easing of French monetary policy. Indeed the easing of policy, by promoting a faster recovery, will accelerate the improvement in French public finances. This plan of action could mean a dip meanwhile in the French franc against the Deutschmark – but it should be temporary only and reversed by the key year of 1998 when the final decisions are taken (including the conversion rates of each currency into the euro) about proceeding to Stage 3 (monetary union). And the extent of the franc's

8   The euro cake falls flat
Source: Hachfeld, *Le Monde*, January 1996.

immediate fall against the mark could be very modest if the Bundesbank itself starts to ease policy substantially. (Indeed, economist Jean-Paul Fitoussi was advising Chirac that France should proceed with unilateral interest rate cuts on the basis that the Bundesbank would soon follow suit, especially if the mark started to rise against the franc.)

The proposal might not, of course, have been accepted, if Kohl had bowed to Tietmeyer's advice. The success of the negotiation would have depended as always on an element of bluff and counter-bluff with its inherent risks. In any event, the hypothetical strategy could not even get off the ground given the uncompromising and unco-operative attitude of Claude Trichet (now governor of the Banque de France). As the franc slipped through summer 1995 on growing concern about the French budgetary situation (and the associated risk that European Monetary Union might be delayed), Trichet pushed up interest rates in its defence – declaring that he would only cut rates if indeed the government instituted budget austerity. In principle Chirac could have stood firm against Trichet's blustering tactics and told him that there would be no budget cuts unless the Banque de France accompanied these with deep cuts in interest rates (not just reversing recent rises). But a head-on battle of brinkmanship between the government and the Banque de France would in itself have been a high-risk strategy both from an economic and a political standpoint. In practice, Trichet had the new government in a corner.

And so, following the reassurance from Kohl, the new Chirac administration proceeded with its budget austerity measures, the French franc returned towards its ERM midpoint, Trichet reversed his earlier tightening of monetary policy and joined in subsequent Bundesbank easing. At the Madrid Summit (December 1995), it was resolved that the EU Council would decide in the first half of 1998 on the basis of economic convergence tests for 1997 which countries were eligible for entry into EMU starting on 1 January 1999. Meanwhile the industrial strife and poor economic performance in France which followed the budgetary and monetary decisions of autumn 1995 became major elements in the defeat of Prime Minister Juppé's government in the spring 1997 parliamentary elections.

Chirac continued to tread a path of no strong resistance to German demands – starting with the agreement at Madrid (December 1995) to jettison the name ecu in favour of euro for the new European currency. In contemporary political cartoons, Chirac, in actual fact a tall man, was portrayed as a dwarf alongside Kohl. In May 1996, when Tietmeyer with the aid of Lamfalussy effected their coup at the European Monetary

Institute, installing Duisenberg as the next president (and so the likely first president of the European Central Bank – see Chapter 1), Paris made no immediate protest. (That came later, in spring 1988 when EMU was already in the bag!) Also, in the course of 1996, France yielded to German demands for a Stability Pact reinforcing budgetary discipline under monetary union. (The demands became more strident when in May Otmar Issing declared that the existing budgetary rules were not strict enough to secure price stability.) The one major concession that France obtained was that fines on countries that defied the Stability Pact should not be automatic but decided upon by the EU Council of Ministers. The final form of the Pact was almost completed at the EU Summit in Dublin (December 1996).

Reinforcing the clamour for a Stability Pact from the German side was the sudden increase in probability during the course of 1996 that Italy would become a founder member of EMU. The dangers of Italian membership became the focal point of German doubts about monetary union. That was indeed a fault of vision, as future events were to demonstrate. The much bigger threat to prosperity and ultimately to monetary stability came from the possibility that the mark would enter EMU at an overvalued level, where the now high-cost and low-investment opportunity German economy would suffer mass unemployment. (See Chapter 3, p. 84, for a discussion of the Bundesbank's later attempt in August 2003 to claim that the Deutschmark was not in fact overvalued when it was converted into euros at the end of 1998.)

9   Ecu or euro?

Source: Hachfeld, *Le Monde*, October 1995.

Most Bundesbankers (including Tietmeyer) had long taken the view that if monetary union were indeed to occur it would be best that it were narrow (France, Germany and Benelux) rather than wide (including Spain, Portugal, and Italy). As late as late June 1996, Ernst Welteke assured his fellow-citizens that Italy had no chance of becoming a founder-member of EMU. His assurances were not widely believed by a public that was dominantly antagonistic to the whole enterprise. A Forsa opinion poll in June 1996 found that 44 per cent of Germans were opposed to union and a further 40 per cent wanted it delayed. A new adverse influence was the deterioration in German public finances and looming tax rises together with spending cuts to meet the Maastricht yardsticks. In April (1996) the six leading economic research institutes questioned whether EMU should go ahead on schedule. Lower Saxony State Premier Gerhard Schröder, a leading contender for SPD leadership, supported calls for delay. Chancellor Kohl sought to squash any possible groundswell in his own party away from EMU by declaring in June 1996 that he would lead it into the next Bundestag election (autumn 1998).

Italy and Spain bang at the door, autumn 1996

Kohl's mission of seeing EMU through to its completion was now leading him into key negotiations with Spain and Italy. In the Italian General Election of April (1996) the Olive Tree Coalition (left-centre) had defeated the euro-sceptic (centre-right–far right) coalition under Prime Minister Berlusconi. The new prime minister, Romano Prodi, soon (July) expressed his determination that Italy should be amongst the founder-members of EMU, warning that severe budget tightening lay ahead. Around the same time, the new Spanish coalition government under Prime Minister Aznar (which emerged from the defeat of the Socialists in the March 1996 elections) announced its strategy aimed at joining EMU from the start.

In terms of the budgetary criteria, Spain was more eligible for entry than Italy. Yet Rome insisted that Italy as itself a founder member of the EC should not enter monetary union behind Spain. Though the entry bids of the two countries emerged around the same time they were in part competitive. Newspaper commentaries suggest that in September (1996) Prodi did seek to form a common negotiating position with Aznar, pressing Germany to accept some softening of entry conditions. That would have been consistent with advice which Banca d'Italia Governor Fazio was giving. Back in July 1996, Fazio had warned against a crash course to EMU entry, saying that austerity would be damaging to the Italian economy.

Aznar, however, pressed ahead on his own, meeting with Chancellor Kohl in mid-October. Prodi was quick to realize what was happening and that Italy could be left behind by Spain in the race to join EMU at its start. The Italian prime minister sought an urgent meeting with the German chancellor and came to Bonn just two days later, well-armed with a severe budgetary package. A swingeing euro tax was to be the means of bringing the Italian budget deficit down to the Maastricht benchmark level. Prodi expressed his concern about the negative commentary on Italy's entry prospects emanating from the Bundesbank and the German Finance Ministry. Kohl assured Prodi of his support for Italy's efforts to become a founder member of EMU, but without giving any guarantees. The chancellor informed Prodi of Bundesbank President Tietmeyer's insistence on Italy first re-joining the ERM by the end of the year and at an exchange rate which did not leave the lira at an over-competitive level. That stipulation was consistent with Tietmeyer's general concern – as evidenced in negotiations with France – that the mark should not be overvalued in the run-up and entry to EMU. (The concern was well-justified in terms of the entry rate, if not in terms of allowing some scope for monetary flexibility in the pre-entry period. Indeed, at least with hindsight, Tietmeyer can be criticized for not insisting that the French franc and the lira should reach substantially higher levels than those actually reached prior to the launch of EMU.)

In the marketplace, the dramatic narrowing in the spread of Italian government bond yields over German during the second half of 1996, and particularly following the Kohl–Prodi meeting, demonstrated that probability assessments of EMU including Italy from the start had increased sharply. New strength of the Swiss franc versus the Deutschmark illustrated the same point, and indeed some commentators suggested that the overall recovery of the US dollar could have been due in part to fears of a soft euro. The passage of an austerity budget through the Rome parliament and the re-entry of the lira into ERM (at a rate which valued the Italian currency somewhat more strongly than what Prodi was bargaining for) in November 1996 provided further momentum to the so-called convergence trades (out of German bonds into Italian and Spanish bonds).

Accountants help to smooth the final lap, 1997–8

Just as the probability of EMU emerging in wide form increased in late 1996, so did the probability fall of the EMU train stalling due to French or German inability to meet the Maastricht budgetary criteria on time.

Back in the summer of 1996 doubts had still been running high about whether even the determination of Chancellor Kohl and President Chirac to see the project through would be sufficient in the face of still weak public finances. In June 1996 the OECD secretariat had warned that the French budget deficit would still run at around 3.75 per cent of GDP in the crucial next year (1997). Two long-time advocates of monetary union, Raymond Barre and Giscard d'Estaing, had criticized (June) the headlong rush without enough attention being taken of the real economy.

In November 1996, the EU statistics agency, EUROSTAT, ruled that it would consider valid a French accounting trick in calculating the budget balance for 1997 – and the EU Commission promptly accepted the ruling. The fudge concerned the forthcoming privatization of France Télécom (slated for 1997) and the transfer of that company's pension fund into the French Treasury in exchange for the government paying the future pension obligations as they arose. The transfer was put in excess of 0.5 per cent of GDP.

10   France and Germany in euro embrace
Source: Hachfeld, Cartoon Exhibition, Paris, April 1997.

If France could get away with an accounting trick, why not Italy with its euro tax fix (which involved not just a real increase in tax but also prepayments)? And surely there was scope for Germany to also do some creative accounting? (In fact, Finance Minister Waigel did announce plans in 1997 to use gold reserve revaluation profits to reduce the deficit, but abandoned these under Bundesbank pressure.) Many market-participants and commentators saw the EUROSTAT ruling as the final fix of the engine that should see the struggling euro train through to its final destination on time.

There were still, of course, some frictions, but none of these could be seen even by contemporaries as terminal dangers. In early 1997 there was some speculation in the German press about a Grand Coalition being formed between Schröder in the SPD and Biedenkopf in the CDU with the aim of delaying EMU. But Schröder was under attack from Lafontaine for his euro-sceptic stance, and results from regional elections in Baden Würtemberg the previous year showed that attacking the euro could be a vote loser (the SPD had fought that election on a euro-sceptic position and had done badly). And Biedenkopf was a long-time maverick commanding no purse-strings. There was some irritation in the German press in February 1997 about a comment from Giscard d'Estaing that the end of the Deutschmark had long been a strategic aim of France, but the ripples did not run deep.

The spring 1997 elections in France brought a small jolt in the final lap, but no more than that. The new Socialist government brought back into power senior officials in Mitterrand's Europe team. Who could believe that they were about to jettison the prize that was now so near? Never mind that the new prime minister, Lionel Jospin, widely seen as a Socialist party aparatchik, had made a few provocative comments during the campaign. In fact the Socialists had laid down four conditions for continuing with EMU: Spain and Italy to be founder members, a dynamic interpretation of convergence criteria, an economic council to balance the power of the ECB, and a growth chapter to the Stability Pact. Spain and Italy were on the verge of boarding the first carriage in any case. The convergence criteria were already being interpreted creatively so why not dynamically? An economic council to balance the power of the ECB in any real sense was going to remain a no-no, given adamant German opposition to anything that smacked of lessening central bank independence. But why not have a meeting once a month of finance ministers from EMU countries and sometimes invite along the ECB president? That was the framework of the so-called euro-Group which emerged at the start of EMU and convened normally one day

11 I bet 10 : 1 on the success of the euro
Source: Chappatte, *International Herald Tribune*, May 1998.

before each regular meeting of EU finance ministers. And whilst on the subject of cosmetics, what about changing the name of the Stability Pact to 'Growth and Stability Pact' and adding a chapter containing a wish list on employment and growth but no real substance?

The final lap through winter 1997/8 and spring 1998 went without further hitch. At the end of March 1998 the Bundesbank published its report on EMU and gave its assent to a wide-EMU starting at the start of the following year. Chancellor Kohl could surely expect as much from his favourite and well-promoted economics official. It was surely no surprise to anyone that the EU Commission found all the applicant countries eligible for immediate entry. In April the German constitutional court ruled against a last-ditch appeal from EMU opponents. And in early May the EU Council gave its final go-ahead. Just before that, Jacques Chirac, confident now that EMU was a done deal, at last risked an act of defiance against German will. The French president declared that it was unacceptable that the present president of the EMI, Wim Duisenberg, should automatically become the first president of the ECB, not least because he owed his position to a central bankers coup in 1996 rather than deliberate choice by the EU Council. Chirac proposed that Claude Trichet should be the first president instead. An informal agreement emerged whereby Duisenberg would voluntarily retire around half way through his eight-year term and be succeeded by Trichet.

On 1 July, the nameplate of the EMI was taken down and replaced by that of the ECB. A batch of operating decisions was taken in the following six-month interim period until the start of European Monetary Union – including the inflation target (2 per cent as measured by the euro-area CPI), dual pillars of policy-making (inflation target and money supply guidelines), secrecy (no release of minutes about policy-making discussions), seating plan around the policy-making table (Bundesbank president to the right of the ECB president), voting (no requirement for formal votes on policy-action) and much more.

No doubt as the champagne bottles popped at the official celebrations on New Years Eve 1999, hard-worked ECB officials felt proud that the destination had been reached on time. Wim Duisenberg was there, as ever, with his camera ready to take snapshots of history in the making. So far the history was one of over one million economic victims, most of all in France, in a long journey pursued under many different banners. But on this day of celebration the architects and the chief functionaries spoke no words of remembrance for the victims. And it was no different at a celebration lunch on 4 January 1999, at the French

12   Will the euro contraption fly?
Source: Hachfeld, *Neues Deutschland*, May 1998.

Finance Ministry. The host, Socialist Finance Minister Strauss-Kahn had invited all French politicians and senior civil servants who had played a role in 'making the euro' (most leading figures of the centre-right, including Raymond Barre, Giscard d'Estaing and Edouard Balladur, had chosen not to come, but there amongst the crowd were Claude Trichet and Michel Camdessus). Yes, the destination had been reached. But how long would the peoples of Europe collectively decide to stay at the point to which they had been brought? Much would depend on whether the years to come brought economic prosperity or hardship.

5
Way Back, Way Forward

However strong the case was against European Monetary Union and against the forced pace of the journey there, it failed to prevail. The grounds for that failure will long be the subject of historical, economic and political analysis. But that is not the end of the matter. The union consists of sovereign states. Any of these might decide in the future to leave the union either unilaterally or in combination. And any member governments can try to obtain the necessary support for effecting amendments to the Treaty of Maastricht or for issuing new EU directives that would bring important changes in the way that the union is run. In sum, whether monetary union should be created and how rapidly has been replaced by the question as to whether it should continue to exist and if so with what modifications to its architecture.

None of this is to slight the importance of the act of creation. Now that the union is here and established the burden of proof on those who would modify or destroy it is greater than on those who once sought to prevent it happening. During the years before creation the advocates of union had to justify not just the ultimate aim but also the economic costs of the journey. Campaigners for separation, dissolution or reform, have to justify the waste in economic resources of effecting a further change of currency regime, even if they can demonstrate that the new one would be an improvement on EMU in its present form. Separations and dissolutions, as we have seen in Chapter 3, are indeed feasible, but not without cost. On the other hand, the campaigners have a growing body of actual evidence from the operation of monetary union so far on which to base their case. They are no longer limited to the hypothetical scenarios drawn up by EMU opponents in the years before its launch and which could have been dismissed as implausible. Evidence is also accumulating on the question of whether European non-members of monetary union can prosper despite their retention of currency independence.

Existential risk of monetary union without political union

Decisions to change monetary regime cannot be separated from wider political considerations. On purely economic grounds, for example, a case might be compelling that New York City should be a separate currency area from the rest of the USA. The periodic booms and bust in the financial sector might have less acute and wasteful spill-over effects into the wider city economy if there were a New York Dollar (NY$), distinct from the US dollar. During periods of boom New York interest rates would rise relative to US interest rates and the NY dollar appreciate versus the US dollar. The price of real estate in NY dollars during the boom phase would rise by less than in US dollars. The jump of the NY dollar and tightening of New York monetary condition in the early stages of boom would mean that the extent of any real estate bubble forming would be less. And similarly in the aftermath of the bubble, the fall-back in real estate prices and wages (both measured in New York dollars) would be less as the New York dollar declined against the US dollar and New York interest rates fell steeply.

A similar case could be made with respect to most great metropolitan cities. And the argument can be buttressed by a longer-term consideration. In some metropolitan cities the rate of productivity growth and investment opportunity might be consistently higher than in the wider economy (with the superior productivity growth concentrated in the 'export' sector). If so, one currency for all would mean persistent upward pressure on the price level (and nominal wage level) of the metropolis relative to that of its hinterland. And along with that persistent upward pressure would probably go a cycle of bubbles in the real estate market as residents in the metropolis saw this as the main hedge against inflation. Where the metropolis has its own currency (with the metropolitan central bank pursuing a target of near price level stability), this would rise to a considerable premium on the basis of future expected rapid productivity growth. The cumulative overall rise in real estate prices would be less (even when measured in the non-metropolitan currency) given a higher prevailing level of real interest rates (than would be the case if the metropolitan area were in monetary union with the rest of the country) and the absence of demand for an inflation-hedge. Moreover, residents in the non-metropolitan area could save partly in the metropolitan currency were they concerned to hedge a future possible relocation into the metropolitan area. (Residents of the metropolitan area could hedge with respect to a future move into the non-metropolitan area by holding a share of their investment portfolio in its currency.)

But New York and other great metropolises belong generally to political federations or unitary sovereign states (for example, the situation of London in the UK). The exceptions in modern times have been Hong Kong (prior to its reversion to Chinese sovereignty in 1997) and Singapore. Further back there was Danzig in the inter-war period. As a technical – but none the less important – point, metropolises (other than the exceptions just mentioned) do not even have their own regional reserve bank within a wider reserve system. New York City is just one district in a much wider area that forms the Federal Reserve District of New York. A political federation typically has rules in any case where the federal government is responsible for certain national functions (including sometimes the issuance of money). A constitutional amendment – to be approved in a, say, two-thirds majority of all states – might be necessary to allow monetary separation. The political drive behind monetary separation would inevitably smack of national disintegration. Could a regional political party seriously campaign for a separate currency without being attacked from all sides for having a secret agenda of ultimate political separation? A purely technical argument about the economic benefits of a separate currency would hardly bring out the crowds at a local election!

In some federations, there is one state where currency separation might be popular on the back of a political separatist movement (for example, Quebec *vs.* Canada or Scotland *vs.* UK). But in these cases the economic argument for a separate currency is quite weak. The popular view would most likely be that all the economic upset of currency separation might be acceptable as part of a deal for creating a national state but not as an end in itself. In the case of the US, political separatism is not a live force in any state or city. Even if a strong economic case could be made for a regional currency, voters would most likely reject it on political grounds (as eroding the ties that make the USA one country and melting pot).

It is quite different in the case of European Monetary Union. If a strong economic case could be made in one country for leaving the union there might not be much counterweight from qualms that this would erode the political fabric of Europe. Yes, in the run-up to EMU hopes that this would be the catalyst to political union enthused substantial numbers of voters in some countries. But if these visions of political union continue to fade, economic realism is likely to prove decisive in any electoral test on the future of monetary union. (Indeed if there is growing political disunion – with bitter differences in foreign and other policies where the European states still remain sovereign – then the economic case for separation or dissolution might win voter support for non-economic reasons.) There is no political federation or confederation as yet in Europe – and there may never be one. The EU is a supranational organization with specified functions – not a sovereign national entity enjoying the almost total loyalty of its citizens, such as the USA, or Switzerland.

Monetary union would survive in the USA or Switzerland – an example of a federation and confederation respectively – even if a convincing case were made that economic prosperity of the whole and each part would increase with separation or dissolution. A benign and enlightened government in Washington or Berne that drew up a plan for regional currencies to replace the national currency would most likely face electoral disaster if it proceeded to implementation – never mind the weight of hypothetical economic evidence in its favour.

Suppose a political union comes into existence where regional currencies already circulate and there is a powerful economic case to preserve them. Monetary integration might nonetheless prove unstoppable due to an overwhelming political logic. That is what happened in the case of German reunification, where Chancellor Kohl swept aside a separate currency regime for the East in the interests of a quick victory for his party in the new Länder (see Chapter 2). If there had been no monetary union in Europe and yet in the far distant future a political federation of European states were to emerge, could the independent currencies survive, or would an inner logic operate, as in the German case? This last question is unanswerable without knowing the exact circumstances of the move towards political union. But it is highly plausible that at least one major European party would include in its programme the aim of monetary union.

The examples of how difficult it is for political federations or confederations to tolerate in their midst more than one money highlight a general weakness in some euro-propaganda. It is a familiar argument of EMU apologists to say – look, all these problems under discussion can also be identified in the US economy. There have been regional depressions and booms in Texas or California, and these have given rise to a dispersion in regional price-level developments similar to those observed during recent years between countries in the European Monetary Union (see OECD *Economic Survey: euro-area*, 2003, for the latest evidence). So why is there so much fuss about continuing high inflation in Spain or the possibility of falling prices and wages in Germany? (And in any case, dispersion of regional inflation rates might be a sign of a well-functioning price mechanism to deal with regional imbalances. Greater dispersion does not inevitably mean greater pain.)

One answer is that economic strains inside the European Monetary Union can raise existential danger for the euro. The political costs of monetary union falling apart as perceived by electorates in the European member countries (duly taking an average of the spectrum ranging from committed Europeans to nationalists) are much smaller, if indeed they can be said to exist, than in the case of Switzerland or the USA. Hence Swiss or US electorates would be willing to support monetary union at a level of demonstrated economic cost which in Europe would bring about its demise. In contrast, the continued existence of sovereign European states, each with their own regional central bank (as a member of the European System of Central Banks) and national political parties, makes the disintegration of monetary union an eminently practical proposition.

The plunge of the euro and its subsequent rebound, 1999–2003

Does the experience so far of monetary union provide us with clues as to where the battle-lines in the future will be drawn between campaigners for reform, dissolution, and separation? A first point is that the behaviour of the exchange rate of the euro to date tells us very little in itself about potential problems ahead. The search for clues has to be more sophisticated than reading the currency charts. To many contemporary commentators the 30 per cent plunge of the euro against the US dollar and Japanese yen from its launch in January 1999 through to autumn 2000 was an alarming signal that European Monetary Union had serious teething problems, if not permanent flaws. International investors were said to have no confidence in Europe's new money, and clumsy or contradictory statements from senior ECB officials were interpreted as symptoms of a general malaise. With the passage of time all the day-by-day drama of the euro as it reached all-time lows can be seen as an episode of particularly low-quality market commentaries rather than carrying any message of deeper significance about the sustainability of the new monetary regime in Europe.

Any significant messages for the future came not from the behaviour of the currency but from how the ECB conducted itself through the

13   Dollar balloon grows larger – euro balloon bursts
Source: Hachfeld, *Neues Deutschland*, June 1999.

pseudo-drama that was playing on the market stage. Clumsy comments of little insight from senior ECB officials and the blanket of secrecy which President Duisenberg and his colleagues had decided to spread over their policy-making deliberations all helped to keep the play running. On top, the ECB scored its first modest mistake in monetary policy-making – well within the range of mistakes made by other leading central banks – in under-estimating the inflationary forces which built up through 2000 (exacerbated, of course, by the weakness of the euro). Thus inflation in the euro-area which had been barely 1 per cent p.a. at the launch of the euro was at 3 per cent p.a. two years later. According to the ECB's own measurement scale (inflation target of 2 per cent p.a. or below), a policy error had occurred. A deeper question was whether the fault lay with the wrong choice of measuring scale (should it have been a target range of 1.5–3 per cent p.a. with, say, an average inflation rate of 2.5 per cent p.a. over an entire business cycle) or bad policy-making (failing to meet a target which was eminently sensible).

The driving force behind the euro's plunge was the US bubble economy. The sharp climb in US interest rates and bond yields and the allure of US equity assets, particularly in the information technology sector, to both European individual and corporate investors fuelled the strongest westward flow of capital across the Atlantic since the Reaganomics boom (1983–5). A key difference this time around was that Japan was not alongside Europe as a huge exporter of capital to the USA. Japanese investors, in view of their own bubble-and-bust history of the late 1980s and early 1990s, and of the East/South-East Asian bubble-and-bust of the mid-1990s, were cautious about becoming involved in the US bubble of the late 1990s. And Tokyo's own NASDAQ-led equity market bubble in 1999–2000 drew in huge flows of foreign capital (as domestic Japanese investors liquidated stock holdings) which helped to drive up the yen. In Europe there was similar (but not identical) background music as in the early 1980s. Then the prevailing theme was euro-pessimism (Europe falling behind in high technology and strategically at risk from the deployment of a new generation of Soviet nuclear missiles). Now the pessimism was concentrated on Germany – its failure to undertake economic reforms and the arrival in power (in autumn 1998) of a red–green coalition viewed as unfriendly to business. On top, the civil war in Yugoslavia had demonstrated the military and geo-political impotence of the European Union.

The Deutschmark had plunged in value by almost 50 per cent against the US dollar during the Reaganomics boom without the then Bundesbank President Pöhl or his institution coming under attack for incompetence. But it was obvious then to all that the USA was the main source of turbulence (huge budget deficit and tight money pulling capital in from the rest of the world) as illustrated by the fact that the Japanese yen was broadly as weak as the Deutschmark. And within Europe the Deutschmark had been strong (as the French franc was devalued sharply in the first few years of the Mitterrand presidency and sterling fell back from the pinnacles reached during its brief existence as a petrocurrency).

On this occasion (1999–2000), if the Bundesbank had still been in command of an independent German monetary policy and currency, it would have had a more challenging task in explaining to the German public why the days of the hard Deutschmark were over, at least for some time. It would not have had the handicap of being a new institution facing a sceptical public. In addition, it could have counted on enthusiastic support from the German business world, which had long hoped for an era when the mark would fall to a competitive level (indeed, this yearning has been a major factor in business support for replacing the Deutschmark with the euro).

Undoubtedly the weak euro pleased many businesses across the euro-area world – but this did not translate into political support. Finance ministers and prime ministers in the euro-zone countries

became growingly alarmed by the weak euro – sensing popular dissatis-
faction with the new currency's performance. Unease about the new
monetary regime – surely to be expected given the revolutionary nature
of the change – was increased by the euro's fall in value. Would the new
currency be as safe as their political leaders had maintained? European
governments saw electoral advantage in making an easy scapegoat of
Wim Duisenberg – why did he not turn up to explain the situation to
euro group finance ministers, and why did he have to make such a
botched attempt at currency market intervention? If their fellow-
citizens were anxious, please understand that their anger should be
addressed to Duisenberg and his colleagues. In general, however,
European finance and economics ministries were ambiguous towards
the situation of a weak euro. These first two years (1999–2000) were
prosperous times again for the euro-area after the various crises on the
journey towards EMU. In particular, employment growth was now
remarkably strong and unemployment fell sharply, most of all in
France, but also in Germany.

There was a gap of around two years between the bursting of the US
equity market bubble together with the sharp slowdown of the US
economy starting in autumn 2000 and the subsequent sustained recovery in the euro. One factor in this delayed reaction of the euro was a
high degree of optimism until late spring 2002 that the US economy's
recession in 2001 was just a 'pause for breath' in a continuing strong
long-run economic upturn. That optimism was finally shaken by the
rapid fading of the economic rebound starting in winter 2001/2 from
the trough following the September 11 terror attacks. A second factor
was the negative surprise of the euro-area economies themselves falling
into recession or near-recessionary conditions. In fact the economic
downturn in Germany revealed itself to be as severe through late 2000
and 2001 as that in the USA. This contradicted the EMU propaganda.
One of the big advantages of monetary union, so its advocates had
claimed, was to make Europe more independent of economic shocks
emanating from the USA. So what had gone wrong?

The architects of EMU had had in mind US monetary or fiscal shocks
that drove capital flows into or out of Germany in particular, given the
Deutschmark's role as the principal alternative investment money to
the US dollar. Resulting exchange rate shifts between the Deutschmark
and other European currencies had on some occasions been a disturbing
factor for the German and other European economies. The architects
were also aware of instances where a bold counter-cyclical policy by one
European economy had floundered due to the failure of other European

countries to follow suit, and so the result had been an intra-European currency crisis. In the new regime, the ECB could decide on a bold counter-cyclical policy for all.

In practice, neither of these past experiences was of much help in understanding how European economies would respond to the latest US shock (2000–1). This time if capital were to flow back from the USA in the wake of the bubble's bursting, it would not have concentrated on the Deutschmark, even if it were still in existence. Germany was now the sick economy of Europe. In principle the ECB was in a position to follow a policy of aggressive stimulus in response to the US bubble-bursting. But in practice the low inflation target which the ECB had set itself, the unexpected degree of inflation divergence (high inflation in the Netherlands, Spain and Portugal, for example, and to a lesser extent in Italy), and unfavourable food price shocks, meant that the ECB drew back from taking bold steps in counter-cyclical monetary policy.

Finally, this latest US shock to hit Europe was based to a larger extent than previous ones on non-monetary factors and unleashed forces that would have dragged the euro-area along regardless of the particular monetary regime in place. The European economies had experienced their own bubble, now burst, in the telecommunications sector (indeed, the advent of the euro may have provided some gas for the bubble by making it possible for the major European telecom companies to borrow massively in the new euro corporate debt markets). European companies had played a significant part in the US bubble through takeover of American companies, and its bursting seriously affected their cash flows and valuations – meaning a knock-on effect with respect to their domestic spending plans. Germany, as an exporter specializing in the production of capital goods, was bound to be particularly hard hit by the first co-ordinated worldwide economic downturn since the mid-1970s, whose key feature was a downturn in business capital spending. Finally, there was the coincidence of a further collapse in the German construction sector, which had been in long-term decline since the peak of its bubble-type boom (exacerbated by generous tax incentives to help develop East Germany) in 1994–5.

The disappointments of experience, 1999–2003

The failure, nonetheless, of Europe's new monetary regime to provide protection against recessionary forces unleashed by the bursting of the US bubble economy in 2001 was undoubtedly a minus point to be considered in any ultimate public trial in a member country. (This would take the form of a public debate as to whether to remain in EMU or whether to launch a major reform effort.) Another minus comes from tentative evidence suggesting that a single monetary policy across the whole euro-area is imposing considerable costs due to substantial economic divergence between the member countries. Residential real estate booms in Spain and Holland (the fourth and fifth largest economies respectively in the euro-area) went along with strong private consumption and a strong rise in the price level in both countries during the years 1999–2002. (The Dutch real estate bubble which saw prices treble through the 1990s was already beginning to burst in 2002. Spanish house prices, which doubled between 1998 and 2003, seemed to be stabilizing by late 2003.) From January 1999 to mid-2003 the Dutch and Spanish price levels rose by a cumulative 14 and 16 per cent respectively, compared to a 6 and 8 per cent cumulative rise in Germany and France respectively.

If Spain and the Netherlands had had still independent monies then they would have appreciated versus the Deutschmark during the period of boom, with Spanish and Dutch interest rates well above German. Once the real estate markets cooled, then the Dutch and Spanish currencies would have fallen in line with interest rates. Instead, under monetary union, the Netherlands and Spain experienced a relatively rapid rate of wage and price inflation (concentrated in their non-traded goods and services sector) during the heyday for the real estate markets and consumer spending. What happens afterwards is problematic. The spike of wages and prices during the boom period could leave both economies exposed to extra-tough competition in their traded goods and services sector with no relief any more from strong demand in the domestic sector. A prolonged period of stagnation could be the result, during which the previous wages and price level spike would be reversed to some extent. Already in the first half of 2003 the Netherlands had indeed fallen into a painful recession, with Wim Duisenberg admonishing Dutch labour for making excessive wage claims. Then in October 2003 the Dutch government announced a 2-year wage freeze. The lower cost way back to equilibrium of a fall in value of the Dutch and Spanish currencies is blocked by the barrier of monetary union.

The Italian inflation experience since monetary union is somewhat different yet contains some worrying pointers. From the start of 1999 to mid-2003, the Italian price level rose by 12 per cent (six percentage points more than in Germany). Yet there was no obvious cyclical or asset-market-related story behind that inflation overshoot. Indeed, the tendency noted by the Bank of Italy for Italian industry to lose competitiveness in traditional sectors (due to import penetration from low-cost producers in Asia and Latin America) without any compensating growth in knowledge-based sectors should have gone along with a fall in the equilibrium level of prices and wages in Italy relative to the euro-area average. It seemed to be a case rather of inflation expectations and wage-setting procedures in Italy (most of all in the service sector) being slow to adjust fully to the new monetary regime (EMU rather than a sovereign Italian money). Hence wage-rates rose well ahead of productivity growth despite weak demand. Ultimately there would be a reality check as Italian enterprises in the traded goods and services sector found their profit margins increasingly eroded by an unfavourable cost structure. They would start to modify their wage-fixing procedures. The subsequent adjustment back to equilibrium could be economically painful.

Germany, of course, has been at the opposite end of the pole to the Netherlands and Spain, suffering a weak real estate market and a slump in its construction sector during the first few years of monetary union. On top of that, Germany, in entering monetary union, had high costs in its manufacturing sector, the main export base, left over from the unification boom and the deep flaws in the earlier monetary union between West and East Germany. If Germany had still had its own currency it would have fallen against the other European currencies during the years 2001–3, and may not have even rebounded against the US dollar. German interest rates would have been at or near zero. Instead the German economy has been subject to deflationary pressures, which, given the normal rigidities of prices and wages, have been reflected in weak or zero output growth. During the years 1999–2003 the cumulative growth of real GDP *per capita* in Germany is estimated at three percentage points less than in France.

Prolonged periods of weak growth in some member countries due to the abandonment of national monetary independence and a still high exposure to US economic shock are unfavourable findings from the experience of the union to date. But in themselves they are hardly enough to bring about a major trial (a national debate on continued entry or major reforms). For that to happen, the weaknesses described would need to be much worse and long-lived. It may be that before a trial can take place there has to be the equivalent of a 'Marie-Antoinette necklace affair' – some provocation to public opinion not directly related to but tangential to the economics of monetary union. The provocation has to be more serious than the rumpus in Italian–German relations in early summer 2003 (Italian politicians including the prime minister making stereotyped negative comments about Germans and receiving a public rebuke from the German chancellor). Corruption or other types of malpractice at the ECB could provide the spark, especially if the alienation of European central bankers from their fellow-citizens were to deepen. And there has to be a mainstream political party in one or more member countries ready to follow the cue.

Political alienation of the ECB

The potential alienation of the ECB from its public is indeed one factor that increases the likelihood of it becoming a target of populist attack. Alienation and the existential danger this might pose to the euro are perhaps the biggest issue in the long-running public discussion of how to increase accountability and transparency. From its inception liberal critics have charged that the secretive procedures adopted by the ECB during the six months run-in to monetary union (July to December 1998) are a disgrace. The European governments should not have left these important questions regarding openness to be resolved by the central bankers themselves.

The occasional self-justifications for, or denials of, secrecy from ECB board members have satisfied none of the critics. For example, ECB officials point to the comprehensive monthly reports, the press conferences which take place once a month directly following a meeting of the policy-making council, and the periodic appearances of the ECB president before the monetary committee of the European Parliament. But the critics counter that the monthly report reads like a collection of bland communiqués, that the press conferences are at best a sleep tonic, and European Parliament hearings are superficial and ill-informed. In defending the decision not to publish minutes of meetings or hold votes before any policy-action, ECB officials have hinted that this would tend to force discussion along national lines (the Italian central bank president making points popular back home) rather than promoting an exchange of views in which each national central banker speaks as a European.

There is no great puzzle about the inclination of the ECB board to avoid a policy of free information to the public. It took determined action by US congressional committees over several years to cause the Federal Reserve under the chairmanship of Greenspan to become more transparent, and even so the reforms fell well short of those demanded. The Federal Reserve, ultimately answerable to Congress (rather than having its roots in the Constitution), is bound to take serious note of reform drives there. The situation of the ECB in relation to the European Parliament is quite different. The ECB has its roots in the Maastricht Treaty – and any threat of reform would come from the EC heads of state putting forward new treaty provisions rather than from the Parliament. In any case, the European Parliament is not embedded in any national political system and thus, unlike the US Congress, is not close to voters. As a matter of fact the European Parliament to date has not pressed the issue of freedom of information with respect to the ECB.

The economic case for transparent monetary policy-making is weaker than the political. There is no strong evidence that transparency produces consistently better monetary decisions. Transparency did not prevent Chairman Greenspan becoming the cheerleader for the US bubble economy. Indeed congressional committee hearings in the late 1990s on monetary policy became highly deferential sessions of the blind saluting the foolish. The degree of short-term uncertainty that pervades monetary decision-making is so great that good decisions are often made on the basis of bad analysis, and bad decisions on the basis of good. Accountability and transparency, if effective, might at the margin improve the quality of monetary policy, but many decades of experience would be required to demonstrate significantly improved results. Nonetheless, if there is no strong reason to believe that accountability and transparency will produce significantly *worse* analysis and, eventually, policy decisions, there are convincing political grounds, especially in the case of the ECB, for observing high democratic standards. The present low standards could contribute to the long-term existential threats facing European Monetary Union.

A first point is that a small but not insignificant share of the electorate in European countries would be more favourably disposed to European Monetary Union if the ECB followed the highest rather than the minimal standards of open government. Secrecy leads to abuses of power and disrespect for a liberal order. An ECB which followed the highest standards of liberalism would already have won the affection of some European citizens. (Of course, as a matter of political philosophy, it can be argued that the ECB should follow the best liberal practice even if no popular support were to be gained.) Further, a completely open ECB, closer to European citizens than it is when enclosed in the present ivory tower, could less easily become the target of popular anti-euro campaigns in any of the member countries.

Full transparency and explicit voting on all decisions would also bring the ECB closer to the various national electorates. Italian citizens, for example, would be able to see just how effective their own national central bank president was at the council meetings and whether he was doing a good job of putting forward points of relevance to the Italian economy. The idea that the national central bank president should be first and foremost a good European and analyse all situations from a European rather than national perspective is a sure way of alienating the ECB proceedings from the various national European publics.

The national central bank presidents could in fact play a key role in democratizing the ECB and making it closer to the people. An effective Bundesbank president, for example, or indeed a president of one of the small central banks, could flout the secrecy conventions that Wim Duisenberg and others put in place at the start of European Monetary Union. Such a president could reveal in public the proceedings at council meetings, and make speeches defying the consensus line as relayed at press conferences or in the monthly report. His own national political power base would have to be strong to do that – having the support, perhaps, of a prime minister who is a renowned Euro-sceptic or of a strong parliamentary following. Indeed, the national central bank presidents who sit around the ECB table could themselves be subject to regular interrogation by parliamentary committees in their own country – and these committees could bring considerable light to bear on what occurs in the euro tower, thus making it less remote from their citizens.

The personality of central bank presidents – both at the national and European level – is a significant factor in any sustained effort to bring the ECB as an institution closer to the European public. The present appointment procedures have deep flaws in that respect. First there was Duisenberg, appointed in a German-led coup for his quality of being a tame chairman who would accept the authority of the German board member and chief economist, Otmar Issing (see Chapter 4). Duisenberg's image was one of clumsiness, smugness, and didacticism. His frequent lectures on why governments – and in particular the German and French – should reduce their budget deficits and observe the Stability Pact were prudish and superficial. They were hardly likely to win the ECB popularity or respect. The ECB had not been appointed as the guardian of the Stability Pact – and so why was its president lecturing elected governments on budgetary policy? He made no lucid argument as to why budgetary deficits during a severe economic downturn posed any serious threat to the ECB's ability to maintain monetary stability. And he did not answer the criticism that if the ECB had followed a bolder counter-cyclical monetary policy the 'big three' governments (Germany, France and Italy) would have been less inclined to adopt stimulative fiscal policies that contravened the Stability Pact.

The next president, Claude Trichet, came from the elite branch of the French civil service (Treasury division), and was renowned or infamous for his unswerving pursuance of the hard franc policy through the early and mid-1990s, irrespective of the rapidly growing army of unemployed. And the allegations made about his propriety in the Credit Lyonnais affair, albeit ultimately rejected in a criminal trial, had counted against him establishing any direct power base in the form of wide pubic support. The main grounds for his appointment as president had been Jacques Chirac's deal with Helmut Kohl in spring 1998 that he should succeed Duisenberg on the latter's early retirement. Trichet was the only French candidate who could have gained the backing of Chancellor Kohl at that crucial summit. To switch horse in 2003 when France's implicit (unofficial) turn came to appoint the president would have been a risky strategy for the Chirac administration, even though doubtless alternative high-quality French candidates could have been put forward. Other EU countries might have taken the opportunity to question France's right to impose its candidate on the rest of the union. And there was no meaningful reappointment process that would bring the new president closer to the European peoples. Trichet was nominated for an eight-year term with no review (unlike four-year terms for the chairman of the Federal Reserve or five years for the governor of the Bank of Japan).

The personality or beliefs of the president may be less important in the case of the ECB than of a national central bank in terms of how solid a base of respect that institution gains. An ECB president could not reign his policy-making council with the absolute power enjoyed by Chairman Greenspan at the Federal Reserve. A national central bank president who defied his lead or guidelines could be backed solidly by a national political constituency. He or she would be less easily sidelined and driven to retire back into academia, as happened for example with Alan Blinder, vice-chairman of the Federal Reserve in the mid-1990s (see Woodward, 2000).

Nonetheless the personality of the president (or chairperson) is a prominent part of central banking. Notwithstanding de Gaulle's quip that cemeteries are full of indispensable men or Milton Friedman's contention that central bankers would be best replaced by a pre-set monetary control mechanism following automatic rules, a few central bank chiefs in the largest economies loom large in any monetary history of the twentieth century. If Claude Trichet were to follow Wim Duisenberg in lecturing European governments on why they should cut back their budgets, and even strengthen the tradition by appearing to hold back on needed monetary easing until budgetary progress were made, that could bring forward the first trial of the euro.

What to do about the Growth and Stability Pact?

The so-called Growth and Stability Pact is one of the major flaws of the design for European Monetary Union, a fact which has become apparent during its first five years of operation. Experience to date suggests that the mechanisms for enforcement (early warning notices issued by the European Commission when breaches are likely to occur, followed by formal notices to rectify matters when infringements are first recorded, backed by the ultimate threat of non-automatic non-interest bearing deposits or fines) are only partially effective. The small countries have been the most virtuous in general. One exception to that rule was Portugal, but once in breach that country assiduously pursued corrective measures to come back into line with the pact's provisions.

The pact's enforcement mechanisms have been less strictly applied when it comes to the large countries and in a situation of near recession or actual recession. Even so, in the case of Germany, the Federal Government has been able to use the obligations under the Stability Pact as a means of bearing down on state and local governments to make budgetary cutbacks. And in Italy the central government has seen the Stability Pact as a useful external prop for enforcing budgetary discipline. But it is evident that in practical terms the fixed benchmarks in the Stability Pact have lacked flexibility to cope with the severe cyclically induced overshoots in budget deficits brought about by economic downturns. Yes, there would have been more flexibility if governments had pursued stricter budgetary policies during the economic expansion of 1999–2000, meaning that pro-cyclical fiscal policy during the economic downturn would not have brought about breaches of the deficit limits. It was hardly realistic, however, for the founders of the Stability Pact to have imagined that, after the hard fiscal slog to reach the Maastricht targets in 1997, member governments would continue to pursue austerity with no abatement in the first few years of monetary union.

Some defenders of the pact would put the blame for the problems encountered so far largely at the door of Otmar Issing and Wim Duisenberg (and their colleagues in the ECB Council) for having followed too tame a counter-cyclical monetary policy. Then the political pressures to use fiscal policy more aggressively than permitted under the Stability Pact might have been contained. This is another version of the attack on the Greenspan Federal Reserve for failing to have eased policy aggressively enough in late 2000 and early 2001 to deprive the Bush administration of cyclical grounds for pursuing its tax-cutting agenda. But a Stability Pact or any other type of constitutional limit on budget deficits that depends on skilled contra-cyclical monetary policy would indeed be flawed in many economic downturns, given the great imprecision of even the most expert monetary piloting under normal conditions of uncertainty. And in the case of the ECB there is the deep hostility of several leading ECB officials, as we have seen, to activism.

The most fundamental method of dealing with the flawed Stability Pact and with the contribution which it might make to an eventual existential danger for European Monetary Union is to scrap it altogether. Even before the pact was drawn up there was some controversy amongst economists as to whether indeed monetary union required budgetary co-ordination alongside. There were two main arguments advanced for a pact – first, its potential role in enhancing monetary stability and, second, its limiting of potential external costs which one profligate government might impose on other member countries. One stability concern was that if the member countries were loaded with high levels of public debt then maybe in the distant future the ECB would yield to political pressure, notwithstanding its constitutional independence, to reduce the real burden (of the debt) by unleashing an inflation surprise. (An inflation surprise would work best in this regard if the average maturity of government debt was long and fixed-rate in form. Otherwise only a sustained policy of driving money rates well below the rate of inflation – a possible recipe for hyperinflation with its devastating economic and political costs – could bring substantial debt relief in real terms.) After all, the fact that the Reichsbank was independent of government under the Weimar Republic did not prevent the descent of Germany into hyperinflation!

Another stability concern was that, if a crisis erupted in any particular government debt market due to weak public finances and rising risk of default, the ECB might monetize the debt in some degree. (Direct monetization is not possible according to the Maastricht Treaty, but the ECB could support banks that were absorbing large amounts of government debt.) That action might prevent a financial crisis but at the possible cost of driving inflation upwards, from which all union members could suffer. And the ECB-led bail-out of the near-defaulting government could impose additional burdens on all if there were indeed an element of debt write-down. For example, the ECB might roll over short-term credits to banks holding the problematic government debt at below market rates and be a party to the banks accepting less than market rates on renewed lending to the government in trouble. Hence the second type of stability concern contains elements of external costs.

The main external cost considered in the literature has been the squeezing out of business investment spending in all member countries by high interest rates due to a huge budget deficit in one or more large economies or a group of small and medium-sized economies. A related cost is the economic adjustment forced on other countries by a big change in the fiscal position of a large country. For example, a sudden large fiscal expansion in Germany would buoy export sectors in other European countries (which would gain from increased German demand) but their non-traded goods and services sectors would suffer from weaker domestic demand in the wake of higher interest rates.

These types of external cost exist, of course, in some degree with or without monetary union. In the early 1980s large US budget deficits under the first Reagan administration were accused widely of sucking in scarce savings from the rest of the world economy and forcing other countries to raise interest rates to counter the inflation threat from a super-strong US dollar. And the boom in European and Japanese export sectors gaining from strong US demand and from the high-priced US dollar was followed by a subsequent bust. But inside a monetary union, where by definition there is no exchange risk to limit capital flows, and exchange rates cannot play any role in smoothing economic adjustment, the external cost of budgetary policy is particularly relevant.

On the other hand, so long as there is no secret plan to defraud (the country with the large deficit intending to default or withdraw from the monetary union), 'squeezing out' or 'sucking in' are notions are of questionable validity. What is the difference from a French point of view between financing large budget deficits or large private sector deficits in Germany or the USA? All are opportunities for French investors to earn more at the margin than what they could have done from boosting the size of the domestic capital stock. Awarding higher value to domestic investment than to foreign lending as a matter of public policy is dubious and smacks of beggar-your-neighbour-type illogicalities (if every country were to subsidize domestic investment compared to foreign investment, all would be worse off).

On closer examination, the widely expressed stability concerns also contain some fallacies. Both concerns are founded on a free-rider problem, which does indeed exist in principle. The government of one member country in a monetary union might run large budget deficits on the assumption that this will not trigger fears about inflation in the long term so long as all other members desist from such profligacy. And the same government might temper its worries about the possibility of an eventual default crisis in its bond market with the reflection that the ECB would most probably bail it out in the end. But, of course, if many governments exploit these free rides, they will end up as an opportunity to none and a cost to all.

In so far as these free-rider problems are for real, they apply more to the small and medium-size countries than to the large. If Germany were to run up massive public sector debts, these would be significant in terms of the euro-area as a whole. Hence the German government could not escape the consequences of its own budgetary excesses to the same degree as a government of a small country. By the same token, however, the German government in pursuing a profligate budgetary path would impose more potential costs on other union members than would do a small country government. In practice the Stability Pact is based on a perceived need in a union to control free rides by small or medium-size countries and joy rides by the large countries at the expense of all.

With no Stability Pact, other mechanisms could be at least partially effective in limiting the scope for free rides or joy rides. The idea that rising government debts in member countries would bring a consensus of EU governments strong enough to sway the ECB away from its present constitutional mandate (as specified in the Maastricht Treaty) of pursuing price stability, or indeed to change the mandate (by revising the Treaty), is implausible except under highly improbable scenarios (including war or natural disaster). An amendment to the Maastricht Treaty would require unanimity. Some national central bank presidents in the ECB Council might yield to political pressures back home in favour of unleashing an inflation shock, notwithstanding their constitutional responsibilities. But it is highly unlikely that the given presidents would gain sufficient influence over the Council to bring about a breach of its commitment to low inflation, even by stealth. Furthermore, the condition of no bail-out by national governments from the ESCB (European System of Central Banks) could be made absolute, by eliminating, for example, the possibility of the ECB acting as lender of last resort to banks whose government bond portfolios are falling sharply in value.

A strict and explicit elimination of any bail-out possibility could take place only if the possibility of member countries being forced out or withdrawing from monetary union were precisely acknowledged in the relevant legal texts. Ultimately, a profligate government encountering a crisis of confidence in its debt market and with no bail-out possible would have little option but to withdraw and start printing its own money. (See Chapter 3 for a discussion of this type of forced exit from EMU in the illustrative context of a future East European member country in crisis.) Member governments realizing the severity of the default scenario might indeed be less inclined to tread the path of fiscal excess than a nation state with its own currency. In the latter case a default crisis can be pre-empted by monetary financing of the government – still with inflation consequences but without all the adverse costs and political drama of an actual default (including a forced exit from monetary union).

Withdrawal by large members can impose costs on all. (Indeed this type of external cost imposed by budget profligacy was not considered in the pre-EMU literature.) There is the issue of who would redeem the union banknotes circulating in the large country – a potential significant cost on all if not undertaken by the withdrawing country. And then there is the reality that European monetary union without Germany would most probably implode – and all member countries would bear the dissolution costs. The government of the large country might hazard that ultimately the other members would agree to some type of monetary rescue for itself to avoid these costs. For example, the ECB might use a rosy forecast of inflation to provide some monetary accommodation for German fiscal excess. The accommodation could take the form of fostering an unexpected subsequent jump in inflation, reducing the real value of outstanding German government debt. Or an extra degree of stimulus – beyond that consistent with overall price stability in the euro-area (meaning just less than 2 per cent p.a. recorded inflation on present guidelines) – could make it possible for the German government to introduce an austere budget. In sum, in a monetary union without fiscal rules but apparently strict prohibition of monetary financing and clear possibility of expulsion (from the union), the largest country might still impose considerable damage on all.

The existence of a Stability Pact with early enforcement provisions (such as the present regime of fines) might moderate but not eliminate the risk of damage by the largest country (whether a costly bail-out, inflation, or dissolution of the union) and also the risk of a costly shrinkage of the union (via forced withdrawal of a small or medium-sized country). The enforcement provisions against the largest country are essentially the weakest. A small or medium-sized country that breaks all the rules (refusing to pay fines or take heed of demands by Brussels for budget cutbacks) would most likely be forced out of monetary union by market pressures. The existence of the pact might mean that these would start to build up at an earlier point than otherwise, given the publicity attached to warnings by Brussels. The government debt market in the given country would fall sharply on a rising risk of default and its banking system would bear the brunt of a flight of capital on speculation about an imminent exit from EMU. The situation might, however, still be retrievable via the implementation of an austerity package. Without the Stability Pact, by the time the government debt market slumped, it might already be politically infeasible to implement remedial budgetary measures of sufficient force.

Since the largest country, Germany, cannot be driven out of the monetary union without endangering the whole, its EMU partners might well tolerate worse behaviour (than possible for the small country) before imposing fines or applying more severe sanctions. A battle between Brussels and Berlin over sanctions or between Frankfurt and Berlin over monetary policy might in an extreme scenario fuel popular support for a party that had adopted an anti-EMU stance, even bringing it into government. Yet ultimately a German government debt default would be more menacing to the future of EMU than any other government default. A key test for any particular version of budgetary pact between EMU governments is whether in fact it reduces the risk of the way-out scenario of German debt crisis.

The Stability Pact should be drafted with sufficient flexibility to prevent a battle flaring up in a situation of deflationary depression. When the ECB has exhausted all conventional monetary tools towards lifting the euro-area economy out of recession or near-recession (meaning that money market rates are already at zero), and inflation is very low or even negative, then there may be a case for an aggressive fiscal stimulus as part of a co-ordinated assault on deflation by the ECB and member governments. There would have to be a formal mechanism whereby the Euro-Group (of finance ministers) and ECB together could call a state of deflation emergency under which exceptional rules both as regards monetary and fiscal behaviour come into effect.

Of course, sanctions and possible shrinkage or dissolution of the union are not the only or even most important barriers to government fiscal irresponsibility. There are also the same barriers that apply in nation states which issue their own sovereign money. In particular the running up of large budget deficits and rapidly accumulating public debt create anxiety amongst the general public about much higher taxes and spending cut-backs in the future. Fiscal profligacy, even though it might confer some immediate gains could fail to win votes. Equity markets might plummet for similar reasons. The net political result might be the government being swept from power. The government of a large country, as for example Germany, might seek to calm its citizens by predicting that the cost of profligacy will be met in part by other union members. But would that really reassure German voters? Even if other members do eventually carry some of the burden (of present profligacy), what would be the price of that support in terms of inter-European relations and the long-term German economic outlook? For example, Berlin might lose the power to push forward policies of particular benefit to Germany at a European level.

In sum, the case for a Stability Pact to accompany monetary union is soft. Governments might be dissuaded by the pact's first-tier provisions concerning fines from sailing as close as they otherwise might to the danger zone where default and forced withdrawal from the monetary union becomes a plausible future scenario. The early warning system and fines might strengthen the market's power to counter fiscal profligacy whilst there is still a reasonable political prospect of taking remedial measures. And the pact provides a neutral multilateral mechanism (the budgetary division of the EU Commission) for persuading both small and large members to take early action that would avoid the danger of an ultimate separation from or dissolution of the union. The German government can potentially use warnings from Brussels experts (at the EU Commission) as a political expedient for tightening budgetary policy. Direct intergovernmental diplomacy might prove much more difficult in achieving that same aim. Why, for example, should the German government accept lectures on fiscal behaviour from the French government? The suggestion that Paris was dictating German policy might indeed make it more difficult politically for the German government to reverse budgetary course.

The soft case just outlined for the existence of a Stability Pact, in a monetary union where debt defaults and forced expulsion are indeed the ultimate penalties for fiscal profligacy and where there is no question of the central bank (ECB) unleashing an inflation surprise to help governments reduce their real debts, is not trivial. But neither is the case weighty enough to justify rigid rules that severely limit the ability of member governments to pursue contra-cyclical fiscal policies (using both automatic stabilizers and discretionary changes). And the trigger for penalties could be changed from various arbitrary yardsticks to include measures of default risk or expulsion risk. Examples of market measures would include yield and money market rate spreads between the country in question and the average of all other countries in the union. The EU Commission could continue to foster informed awareness in the markets about the fiscal position of each country (and its sustainability), using its treaty powers to extract information from the various national governments. The basic asymmetry, however, could not be changed between the power of Germany and of the small or medium-size countries to flout the rules.

Will a small country be the first to leave?

In practice, to date most small countries in EMU have made a better job of complying with the Stability Pact, both in letter and intent, than the large countries. Unsurprisingly some small country governments resent the inevitably favourable treatment of the large countries. Resentment, frustration at the almost total loss of power in monetary policy-making, and economic circumstances might come together to make one or more of the small countries the first base of a major political force in favour of national withdrawal from EMU. It is a common fallacy to argue that small countries have least to give up in joining monetary union as their pre-union situation was one of being a monetary satellite or maintaining a small national freely floating money which was both high cost and unstable. (The case of small countries and why they may be better off economically outside the union has already been explored in Chapter 1.) According to the same fallacy, monetary independence in its best sense (a liquid currency and fairly stable in terms of domestic purchasing power, including imported goods and services) was never theirs to be had. Surely they are better off with a seat on the policy-making board of the central bank responsible for a large monetary area.

In reality, a small country has considerable potential monetary power on its own – more so in one important respect than a large country. The example of Switzerland illustrates that even the currency of a small economy can rank amongst the leaders in terms of stability (measured with respect to domestic purchasing power). True, businesses in a small economy may be subject to a greater extent than in a large to exchange rate uncertainty. And so the central bank of a small currency might steer policy to a greater degree in the short run guided by events in the exchange market than would the central bank of a large currency. A domestic inflation target, by contrast, might be less prominent as a short-term guide to monetary policy in the small currency country. But if inflation or deflation risks loom large, the central bank of a small independent money can act with decisive impact – by driving its currency up or down respectively in the foreign exchange market. The exchange rate is one of the strongest short or medium term levers of monetary policy, even in the case of medium-size countries (for example the UK). But in the small country case it is all-powerful. As part of monetary union, Belgium, for example, can be dragged into deflation or inflation for periods of many years or even a decade or more. On its own, there is a quick exit from both.

What does the small country obtain in return for giving up its particularly effective exchange rate weapon – and some other benefits of monetary independence (including less possible exposure to fiscal abuse by the largest country in the union, and no requirement to comply with union-wide tax and bank secrecy rules which might curtail its financial sector)? The usual response is a seat at the board and the economic gains of increased trade and international investment that should go along with the elimination of exchange rate uncertainty. The economic gains are open to debate and no doubt will continue to be the object of much inconclusive empirical work for many years to come. It would be hard to put a high value on the board seat under present institutional arrangements. Perhaps the value might rise where the national central bank president by intellect and charisma became an opinion-former in the monetary council and popular with the public both in his own country and outside. Even so, it is not clear that the gains would be any more than an issue of national pride rather than economic substance. In practice present trends in the European Monetary Union point to a further dilution of the already marginal power of small national central bank presidents.

In particular, under the provisions of the Treaty of Nice, national central bank presidents will have voting rights in the ECB policy-making council only on a rotation basis once the European Monetary Union expands to include most of the central and East European countries who join the EU in 2004. According to a proposal made by the ECB in spring 2003, the presidents of the large central banks would have least time off from voting (one year in five), and the small central bank presidents most (but never more than one year in two). Medium-size central bank presidents would vote in eight years out of eleven. According to preliminary proposals made by the ECB, France, Germany, Italy, Spain, and the Netherlands, would all fall into the category of large for this purpose. All other present EMU members (including the smallest, Luxembourg) and some East European entrants would be treated as medium. The category of small would include the Baltic countries, Slovakia and Slovenia. By convention, France, Germany, and

Italy would presumably continue to have one out of the six board member seats.

Future expansion of EMU to the east and north

In economic size (measured at market exchange rates), the combination of all the east and central European countries joining the EU in 2004 is the same small share (6 per cent) of the EU economy on the eve of expansion as were Spain and Portugal together just prior to their accession in 1986. On the basis of PPP exchange rates, the new entrants account for nearly 9 per cent of the total. According to draft proposals, the new EU entrants together with Rumania and Bulgaria (expected to join the EU late in the present decade), once they become members of monetary union, would have aggregate voting power equal to 40 per cent of total national central bank presidents and around 30 per cent of the total council (including board members). That is sufficient to have a bearing on the consensus attitude towards inflation targeting.

In particular, according to the well-known Balassa hypothesis, economies that are rapidly catching up with their more advanced counterparts are likely to have relatively high inflation (if their currencies are at fixed parities to one another). This stems from the much faster rate of productivity growth in the traded goods and services sector than in the non-traded that is typical of catch-up economies. (In most economies, measured productivity tends to rise faster in the manufacturing sector than the services sector – but the differential is particularly large in the case of catch-up economies.) The law of one price means that the prices of traded goods and services (translated into a common currency) will move up or down in step with those elsewhere in the global economy. But the price of output from the comparatively inefficient non-traded goods and services sector in the catch-up economy would rise (albeit from a low starting level) relative to that elsewhere (in already mature economies). If indeed the central and eastern European economies grow rapidly, it should be expected that their inflation rates would be persistently higher – possibly by a margin of 3–5 per cent p.a. – than in the old euro-area. In those circumstances, would the 30 per cent voting bloc of national central bank presidents from the catch-up countries be over-concerned about whether inflation averaged across all union members were somewhat above target? In any case, even the old-member presidents and board members might be convinced by the rationale of adjusting upwards the overall inflation target so as to avoid compressing the effective target for the original euro area to significantly below 2 per cent.

Of course the entry of the central and eastern European countries into EMU could take considerably longer than the minimum of two years provided by the various protocols on the subject. There must be two years of membership in the revamped exchange rate mechanism (a fixed-exchange rate system based on the euro) with no devaluation during that period. The standard convergence criteria – including performance yardsticks on public finances, government debt outstanding, and inflation – must be satisfied. And then there are some overriding more general considerations which would doubtless include an examination of banking sector stability. The present EMU countries will be cautious about assuming lender of last resort responsibilities with respect to the ailing ex-communist segment of the banking industry in the accession countries.

The Deutsche Bundesbank has already sounded the alarm (see *Monthly Bulletin*, July 2003) that problems of instability (poor loan supervision, for example) can also be found in post-communist sectors of the banking industry. In addition, the Bundesbank has cited the low level of financial intermediation generally in the accession countries, and the imperfect arbitrage between money markets there and the euro-area, as grounds for caution before proceeding to EMU membership. Present members would also have to satisfy themselves that the fiscal criteria will indeed be adhered to. Otherwise the European Monetary Union could be faced with a first case of expulsion or forced exit, and with the existing members bearing some of the cost (absorbing, for example, the euro banknote issue from there).

Indications so far are that the central and east European countries will seek to join EMU as soon as possible. Indeed, as a matter of legal principle, they cannot choose to opt out once they satisfy all the conditions for entry. In practice it is hard to imagine that existing members would force an east European country displaying great caution towards entering EMU to accelerate its progress into the union. By far the most important negotiation, in view of economic size, will be with Poland.

The arguments put forward for early membership of EMU by east and central European officials focus on the disadvantages of alternative currency regimes. In particular, membership of ERM-2 (a fixed exchange rate system linking non-EMU currencies in the EU to the euro) might subject them to periodic inflows of hot money in search of high interest rates (generated by rapid economic growth) at limited apparent downside exchange risk. The inflows would exacerbate the tendency for inflation to run higher in the accession countries than in the euro-area. Alternatively, if they opt for a long period of a freely floating currency, speculation on their becoming Tiger economies might push the exchange rate to unrealistic highs which would snuff out the prospect of a growth take-off.

The same officials tend to understate or not mention at all forms of instability which might follow from premature entry into EMU or the growth miracles which have occurred in east or south-east Asia notwithstanding the absence of any monetary union. (Their stock answer to Asian comparisons is to point out the existence of exchange restrictions that sheltered the Tigers there from speculatively driven serious overvaluations of their currency and which could not be applied in the context of the EU. But the existence or efficacy of these restrictions in the various Asian examples is in fact for the most part dubious.) A main form of instability is the likelihood of real estate market bubble. If the given country makes it to tiger status, and yet interest rates are set at the low common rate for the euro-area as a whole, a huge speculative boom could get under way in all real assets (particularly real estate). The effective real interest rate in the tiger economy would be very low and most probably highly negative (given the high rate of inflation there in line with the Balassa effect). Real estate would become subject to huge demand as an inflation-hedge. Most likely a bust would follow, including a full-scale banking crisis. The rest of the euro-area might end up carrying the can or the given country be forced to exit EMU (if the ECB would not act as lender of last resort).

The potential for real estate market or wider economic bubble and bust in the accession countries following their eventual entry to EMU depends in part on the conversion rate (of the national money into euros). A high conversion rate that appears to substantially overvalue the national currency at the point of entry would help to keep the cool despite interest rates now being at the low euro level. The cost, however, of the high entry rate could be substantial in terms of holding back otherwise rapid development of the traded goods and services sector which should be the engine of dynamic growth. Unlike in the negotiations leading up to the launch of the euro in 1999, in further expansions of the euro-area the question of the conversion rate might become central. There would not be a blind acceptance of the latest central parity rate (in ERM) as the appropriate entry rate. Technically, the hard negotiations might be about the central rate that is to apply in the two-year run-in period to monetary union.

The question of entry rate would also be crucial to any serious negotiations that were to get underway between London and Brussels on the UK joining EMU. The UK government is committed to a referendum if and when a final decision in favour of entry is taken. Unlike in the French referendum of 1992, the case to be made by the EMU advocates in the UK would be primarily economic. In France, the pro-Maastricht case turned largely on the need to contain the power of the recently united Germany by deepening European integration. In addition there was the 'Euro-nationalist' theme music of building Europe so as to counter US hegemony. And the idea that France would gain power in the new Europe and the hegemony of the Bundesbank would be destroyed also featured significantly. None of these themes would be relevant or go down well with the UK voting public. The strategy of a UK government seeking to win a euro-referendum vote might well be to convince the majority of the low numbers actually voting that their economic interests would be well served. An easy constituency amongst whom to rally support would be all those who would gain from a devaluation of sterling prior to entry. And then there are the homeowners who could look forward to an immediate cut in interest rates to the lower level in the euro-area than the UK and a possible jump in their main asset's price.

Whether indeed a UK government is seriously able to offer the devaluation prize in a referendum campaign would depend on the result of EMU entry negotiations. Of course there is the option of making a fraudulent offer. The UK government could campaign on the devaluation-based advantages of EMU, win the referendum, and then find that its negotiating partners in Brussels, Berlin and Paris, would not concede a cheap entry rate for sterling. No doubt there would be a face-saving formula for the UK government in that situation to proceed, providing that its parliamentary majority were secure. This pro-EMU strategy could falter however if the anti-EMU campaigners were to expose successfully the at best speculative nature of the devaluation assumption on which the UK government was marketing the case for the UK joining monetary union.

The democratically, and probably politically, sounder strategy for a pro-EMU government in the UK to follow would be to negotiate a whole range of questions, including the important issue of the exchange rate, with its EU partners prior to a referendum campaign. Crucially the UK might seek to get a commitment to reform of monetary union. Technically the EU Council could agree that an inter-governmental conference should be called within one year from the referendum to propose treaty amendments essential to the reform of monetary union. The UK government might delay entry into EMU until the conference were over and an acceptable reform deal achieved.

An agenda for reform

What would an agenda for reforming EMU, most probably in the setting of an intergovernmental conference, include?

An obvious first point would be reform of the Stability Pact – along the lines of reducing or eliminating any loopholes whereby the ECB could bail out governments and switching emphasis to a wide range of advance indicators of fiscal-driven instability. Arithmetic yardsticks and arbitrary restrictions on the scope for following contra-cyclical fiscal policy would be modified or scrapped.

Second, responsibility for enunciating the inflation target consistent with the Treaty's concept of price stability would be broadened out beyond the ECB to include some political input. A Stability Council, consisting for example of the president and vice-president of the Euro-group (of finance ministers) and the president of the ECB together with the chairman of its policy-making council (see point 4 below) would decide on the exact specification of the inflation target, subject to approval by the ECB Council (in an open vote).

Third, the Stability Council, which could be called into session by either the ECB or the euro-group, would be empowered to call a state of deflation alert, subject to ratification by the EU Council. This would occur where money market rates had already fallen to near zero and yet the medium-term economic outlook in the euro-area was for continuing slackness in resource utilization and high unemployment. Under a state of deflation alert, there would be well-defined partial suspensions of the Stability Pact to allow fiscal policy to be used as part of an unconventional policy package to combat deflation. The ECB would also be empowered exceptionally to aggressively buy government bonds and foreign exchange as the means of rapidly expanding the monetary base. The Stability Council would also have the authority to propose to the Council of Ministers an emergency package of measures that would allow interest rates to fall to negative levels. These measures would include some version of forced currency conversion or banknote taxation so that the return from hoarding banknotes fell below zero. (One such proposal was set out by the author in *The Yo-Yo Yen*. The Japanese government would announce that in, say, five years' time 100 old yen banknotes would be converted into 90 new. In the interim the 1:1 exchange of bank deposits into banknotes would be suspended.)

Fourth, there could be reform of the ECB's organizational structure. Alongside the president would be a chairman of the policy-making council who would be one of the five large central bank presidents on a rotation basis. Nominations for ECB board members could be made by any group of finance ministers whose countries' economic weight combined passed a given threshold – say 15 per cent of the total. (That would allow each of Germany, France and Italy to make nominations unilaterally.) The Euro-group of finance ministers would make the final choice as to candidate on the basis of some type of weighted voting (partially to reflect economic size). Three seats on the board would be preserved at all times for nationals of the three largest countries. The term of the president's office would be reduced to four years from eight and he or she could only go forward to reappointment if approved by a majority in the European Parliament. There would be an over-riding provision that where the inflation target is missed by a stipulated amount in either direction (too much inflation or deflation), then the EU Council could dismiss the ECB board and appoint a replacement according to the procedures already outlined.

Fifth would come democratization and transparency. There would have to be a vote at every policy-making meeting. The voting behaviour of each council member, together with a full transcript of policy-making discussions, would have to be published within a month of the meeting. Each council member would have to provide a short summary of the reason for his or her voting decision. A rotation system would be drawn up under which ECB board members made regular appearances before committees in the five largest national parliaments (and once a year in one of the small).

Sixth, the present unclear provisions as to responsibility for foreign exchange market intervention would be replaced by a clear statement that this was not a matter for discretionary action by the ECB. The ECB could intervene only on the authority of a mandate from the Council of Ministers (or euro-group) or exceptionally as a tool of monetary policy under deflationary conditions (see above). In addition, there could be framework rules describing under what conditions the Council of Ministers would authorize intervention (for example, disorderly markets or international liquidity crisis), making clear the overriding principle of a free float for the euro against other currencies.

Seventh, clear principles would be set out for member countries to observe in a unilateral withdrawal from European Monetary Union.

Rules would be established for the case of a general dissolution of the union. The grounds would be stated on which the EU Council could resolve to suspend a country's membership of monetary union (for example, flagrant violation of all its treaty obligations). The political basis for exit provisions to be specified is the non-federal nature of the European Union. The non-provision of a clearly described exit to monetary union smacks of federalism rather than a loose political association of sovereign states. The economic basis – reduction of potential financial instability in the case of separations or dissolution which become unstoppable – has already been highlighted in Chapter 3.

Which government would lead the drive for reform?

In pressing this reform agenda as part of the entry negotiations the UK would find itself in alliance with pro-reform political forces, including some governments, within the present EMU. That might help win agreement to a generous (cheap) conversion rate for the pound on entry. A more important consideration, however, would be the enthusiasm of some European governments to have the UK more fully integrated into Europe, given the implications of this for better relations with the USA. Moreover, the image of the UK government putting itself at the heart of a European debate about the reform of the monetary

14   Only UK prime minister Blair refuses to worship the euro sun
Source: Hachfeld, *Neues Deutschland*, January 1998.

union might indeed win supporters for entry back home. The argument would be that here was an historic opportunity for the UK to improve monetary union, rather than delaying the decision until much later when all flexibility had gone.

A UK government following such a strategy would have a difficult choice as to when to time the ultimate referendum. If the government waited until the inter-governmental conference on EMU reform had come to an end, an unfavourable outcome could jettison a positive (pro-entry) result. And the UK as an uncommitted outsider might not have much influence on the proceedings in any case. On the other hand, in a referendum campaign before conclusion of negotiations on reform the opponents of EMU would simply need to brandish the list of changes demanded as demonstration enough that it was premature to vote yes to joining. The government could attempt to argue in response that a yes vote was crucial to it achieving the reforms – in that those members of EMU who wanted the UK to join would do all possible to prevent the opportunity of the referendum result being squandered (as would happen if the UK government, even armed with a yes vote, decided ultimately against, on the basis of reforms being unsatisfactory).

As of the time of writing (late 2003), there is not much of a basis for speculating that UK entry negotiations, even if they got started, would indeed be the catalyst to important reforms in the union. How could the reform process start from within the present union? One possibility would be the French and German governments together resolving to kick-start reform, putting before the EU Council of Ministers a similar plan to that outlined above. If the French and German economies were to suffer from more years of weak economic performance, the temptations would surely be great for politicians on both sides of the Rhine to lay blame at the doors of the ECB and press the case for reform.

On the other hand, Germany could act alone using strong-arm tactics – pressing a reform agenda with the implicit threat that if other countries were to stall then the Deutschmark could be resurrected and monetary union fall apart. Germany might add to the reform list a requirement that the ECB gives greater weight to German economic conditions than simple arithmetic yardsticks would suggest (the share of Germany in euro-area GDP), and, as we have seen in Chapter 1 (p. 17), there is some theoretical basis for that. (Other suggestions for a German list of reform demands have been made in Chapter 3.) Another less dramatic possibility is that a smaller country takes the initiative, possibly during its periodic presidency of the EU (so long as this continues to rotate), and through powers of persuasion and clever diplomacy moves the reform process forward.

The case of a reform agenda being driven by the spectre of one or more countries deciding to withdraw from EMU or even of the dissolution of the whole carries the risk of considerable financial crisis as the game of bluff and counter-bluff plays out. There are several sets of economic conditions that would provide fertile soil for politicians to begin to make the case for withdrawal. These include for example a long depression in the euro-area economy or, less likely (from the viewpoint of 2003), the outbreak again of high inflation (meaning a big mistake by the ECB). Small or medium-sized countries could make a quick exit in a dash to restore stability. Or one country could find itself in particularly difficult economic circumstances – due perhaps to the collapse of a local real estate market bubble or a structural shift of demand away from its principal exports. Or the German economy might fail to recover from the depression into which it sunk in the early 2000s and from which the quick exits had been blocked by the existence of EMU in its present form.

Fertile economic soil is neither an absolute necessity nor a sufficient condition for separation or dissolution to become real possibilities. The momentum might come from purely political sources. A government might come into power in one country with an agenda which could not be fulfilled within the constraints of monetary union – involving in particular large and persistent deficits in the national budget or a big change (for the worse) in domestic returns to capital. Or opinion might sour in a particular country against the EU in general, including its main federal institution, the ECB.

On the other hand, where commitment remains strong towards the ideal of growing political integration in Europe, then even fertile economic soil would not cause a movement in favour of monetary disintegration to grow. And even where commitment is not strong there are the unique events, coincidences, and personalities, which will play a role in determining the outcome. Does a charismatic and able politician in a member country take up the case of separation as his or her road to power or sustaining of power? And at a crucial juncture does the ECB shoot itself in the foot – either via a serious policy mistake or through revelation of internal incompetence or corruption?

How should investors treat existential risk of the euro?

Should the possibility that separation or dissolution or indeed substantial reform lies on the medium-term horizon for European Monetary Union affect the present behaviour of international investors with respect to the euro? It is indisputable that the euro does indeed bear existential (will monetary union survive?), territorial (will the euro-area expand or decrease substantially in economic size due to new arrivals and departures?) and framework (will the ECB and the constitutional rules of monetary union be reformed?) risks not born by the US dollar. In appraising the risks of euro bonds, for example, issued by governments in each of the member states, there are political risks (relating to separation or default) which the investor would not have to consider in the case of US dollar debts. The possibility of separation and dissolution also goes along with a somewhat higher risk of banking crisis in the euro-area at some far-distant date (as capital might flee the banks in the country where the separation risk becomes significant).

These existential, territorial and framework risks do not at present loom as a significant factor in investor appraisal of the euro. If they were to become more important, their main impact would be to shrink the international use of the euro. Both international borrowers and lenders eschew uncertainty. Whether the overall effect would be to push the euro higher or lower would depend largely on asymmetry of response to risk between international borrowers and lenders and on the specifics of the particular separation, dissolution, or reform scenario which is dominant in the marketplace. The failure of the euro to flourish so far as an international money (in terms of total market share) has little to do with such scenario-building but more to do with the fact that several Asian countries (including China) are anchoring their currencies to the US dollar. Perhaps the enthusiasm of ECB President Duisenberg for Washington's new policy in autumn 2003 of promoting freely floating currencies in Asia (particularly the yuan and the yen) – thereby undermining the Asian dollar bloc – stemmed in part from a realization that the euro could gain thereby in international importance. If so, an unholy alliance between US mercantilists and euro nationalists was behind the debut of the euro-area on the G7 stage at Dubai (20 September, 2003).

Nonetheless, it is one of the many paradoxes of European Monetary Union that its first five years have seen the US dollar gain a degree of worldwide hegemony not seen since the early 1960s. Zero rates, the Lost Decade, and a latent fiscal crisis, have knocked out the yen as a serious global competitor to the US dollar. Germany's prolonged economic decline, due at least in part to the disastrous two monetary unions of the 1990s, have weighed against the euro enjoying the popularity of its predecessor as Europe's principal international money, the Deutschmark.

And therein lies an essential constant. The success of the euro turns on the German economy thriving and Berlin playing by the rules of the game. The French architects of monetary union believed that the new monetary order would eclipse German hegemony in Europe's monetary affairs. The first five years of monetary union have indeed seen German influence at a low ebb. And a French president has just been installed at the ECB for a prospective term of eight years. But, as we have seen, present appearances might be quite deceptive as regards future realities.

Germany has the power, unshared by any other country, to either undo the union, or bring about major reforms, or inflict serious economic damage on its co-members. If the German economy continues to suffer from the existence of monetary union, then Berlin will surely at some point start to flex its monetary muscle. At any point unilateralist fiscal action in Germany (say on the scale of the Reagan or Bush budget shocks), or severe social and political crisis there, could subject European monetary union to considerable stress. Other members would face a no-win choice – either to accept a list of reforms demanded by Berlin or bear the costs of dismantling the union and returning to national currencies. French leaders who in the 1980s and early 1990s drove their country along the long hard road to monetary union bargained on the prizes of greater independence from the USA, reduced monetary hegemony for Germany and new power for France on the European stage. They not only took the wrong turn but overvalued the prizes.

Bibliography

Aeschmann, Eric and Riché, Pascal (1999) *La Guerre de Sept Ans: Histoire secrète du franc fort, 1989–1996* (Paris: Calmann-Lévy)

Alphandéry, Edmond (1998) *La Réforme obligée: sous le soleil de l'euro* (Paris: Grasset)

Amoureux, Henri (1994) *Monsieur Barre* (Paris: Robert Laffont)

Barnavi, Élie and Friedländer, Säul (1985) *La Politique étrangère du Général de Gaulle* (Paris: Presses Universitaires de France)

Bauchard, Phillippe (1997) *Deux Ministres trop tranquilles* (Paris: Belfond)

Brown, Brendan (1978) *The Dollar–Mark Axis* (London: Macmillan)

Brown, Brendan (1986) *Monetary Chaos in Europe 1914–31* (London: Routledge)

Brown, Brendan (1987) *The Flight of International Capital 1931–86* (London: Routledge)

Brown, Brendan (1996) *Economists and Financial Markets* (London: Routledge)

Brown, Brendan (2002) *The Yo-Yo Yen* (Basingstoke: Palgrave Macmillan)

Brunila, Anne, Buti, Marco and Franco, Daniele (2001) *The Stability and Growth Pact* (Basingstoke: Palgrave Macmillan)

Buiter, Willem H. (1999) 'Optimal Currency Areas: Why Does the Exchange Rate Regime Matter?' (Scottish Economic Society Annual Lecture, 1999)

Buti, Marco and Sapir, André (1998) *Economic Policy in EMU* (Oxford: Clarendon Press)

Ca'Zorzi, Michele and De Santis, Roberto A. (2003) *The Admission of Accession Countries to an Enlarged Monetary Union: A Tentative Assessment* (ECB Working Paper No. 216, February)

Chari, V.V and Kehoe, Patrick J. (1998) *On the Need for Fiscal Constraints in a Monetary Union* (Federal Reserve Bank of Minneapolis, Working Paper 589)

Chazal, Claire (1996) *Édouard Balladur* (Paris: Flammarion)

Cobham, David and Zis, George (2001) *From EMS to EMU: 1979 to 1999 and Beyond* (London: Routledge)

Connolly, Bernard (1998) *The Rotten Heart of Europe: The Dirty War for Europe's Money* (London: Faber & Faber)

De Grauwe, Paul (1990) *The European Monetary System in the 1990s* (Harlow: Longman)

Delors, Jacques (1998) *L' Unité d'un homme* (Paris: Seuil)

Deutsche Bundesbank (2003) 'Wege aus der Krise' (*Monthly Bulletin*, March 2003)

Deutsche Bundesbank (2003) 'Die Finanzmärkte in den mittel- und osteuropäischen Ländern vor dem Beitritt zur EU' (*Monthly Bulletin*, July 2003)

Deutsche Bundesbank (2003) 'War der deutsche Konversionkurs beim Eintritt in die Währungsunion zu hoch?' (*Monthly Bulletin*, August 2003)

Dosenrode, Soren (2002) *Political Aspects of the Economic and Monetary Union: The European Challenge* (Aldershot: Ashgate)

Eichengreen, Barry (1992) *Should the Maastricht Treaty be Saved?* (Princeton Studies in International Finance No. 74)

Eichengreen, Barry (2000) *The Political Economy of European Monetary Unification* (New Haven, CT: Westview Press)

Eichengreen, Barry and Ghironi, Fabio (2001) 'EMU and Enlargement', Conference paper, European Commission, March.

European Central Bank (2001) 'Review of the International Role of the Euro', Special paper.

European Central Bank (2001) *The Monetary Policy of the ECB* (Frankfurt).

Fabius, Laurent (1995) *Les Blessures de la vérité* (Paris: Flammarion)

Feldstein, Martin (1997) 'The Political Economy of the European Economic and Monetary Union: Political Sources of an Economic Liability', *Journal of Economic Perspectives*, 11(4): 23–42.

Feldstein, Martin (2000) 'The European Central Bank and the Euro: The First Year', NBER Working Paper No. 7517, February.

Fratianni, Michele and Spinelli, Franco (1997) *A Monetary History of Italy* (Cambridge: Cambridge University Press)

Fitoussi, Jean-Paul (1994) *'Le Débat interdit: Monnaie, Europe, Pauvreté'* (Paris: Arléa–diffusion Le Seuil)

Frowen, Stephen and Pringle, Robert (1998) *Inside the Bundesbank* (London: Macmillan)

Garber, Peter and Spencer, Michael (1994) 'The Dissolution of the Austro-Hungarian Empire: Lessons for Currency Reform', Essays in International Finance No. 191, Princeton University.

Gedmin, Jeffrey (1999) 'Helmut Kohl, Giant', Policy Review, No. 96, Washington, DC: Heritage Foundation.

Hartmann, Phillip and Issing, Otmar (2002) 'The International Role of the Euro', *Journal of Policy Modeling*, 24: 314–45.

Holsman, Robert (1996) *Maastricht: Monetary Constitution Without a Fiscal Constitution?* (Baden-Baden: Nomos)

Issing, Otmar (2001) 'The Single Monetary Policy of the European Central Bank: One Size Fits All', *International Finance* 4(3): 441–62.

Issing, Otmar and Gaspar, Vitor *et al.* (2001) *Monetary Policy in the Euro Area* (Cambridge: Cambridge University Press)

Jones, Erik (2002) *The Politics of Economic and Monetary Union: Integration and Idiosyncrasy* (Lanham, MD: Rowman & Littlefield)

Jonung, Lars (2002) 'EMU and the Euro: The First 10 Years', Economic Papers, No. 165, February 2002 (European Commission, Directorate-General for Economic and Financial Affairs)

Lacouture, J. (1999) *Mitterrand: Une histoire de François* (Paris: Seuil)

Leaman, Jeremy (2001) *The Bundesbank Myth* (Basingstoke: Palgrave Macmillan)

Madelin, Philippe (1998) *Jacques Chirac: une biographie* (Paris: Flammarion)

Marsh, David (1992) *The Bundesbank: The Bank that Rules Europe* (London: Heinemann)

Martinet, Gilles (2002) *Les Clés de la Cinquième République* (Paris: Seuil)

Meier, Gert (1997) *Das Ende der D-Mark: Vision oder Wahn* (Frankfurt: Gie-Tübingen)

Meyret, Romain (1994) *La Face cachée de Jacques Delors* (Paris: Édition Première Ligne)

Miard-Delacroix, Hélène (1988) *Partenaires de Choix? Le chancelier Helmut Schmidt et la France* (Frankfurt: Peter Lang)

Milesi, Gabriel (1997) *Jacques Delors; L'homme qui dit non* (Paris: Édition No. 1)

Muet, Pierre-Alain and Foneneau, Alain (1987) *Reflation and Austerity: Economic Policy under Mitterrand* (Oxford: Berg)

Mundell, Robert A. (1994) 'The European Monetary System 50 Years after Bretton Woods'. Paper presented at Project Europe 1995, Sienna, November.

Mundell, Robert A. (1998) 'The Euro and the Stability of the International Monetary System'. Paper presented at Luxembourg Institute for European and International Studies, December.

Muns, Joaquim (1998) *'Spain and the Euro: Risks and Opportunities'* (Madrid: La Caixa)

OECD (1999) *'EMU: Facts, Challenges and Policies'* (Paris: OECD)

OECD (2000) *'EMU One Year On'* (February)

OECD (2003) 'Economic Survey, Euro-Area' (Paris: OECD)

Paolo, Francesco (2002) 'New views on the Optimum Currency Area Theory: What is EMU Telling Us?' ECB Working Paper No. 138, April.

Péan, Pierre (1994) *Une Jeunesse Française* (Paris: Librairie Arthème Fayard)

Pentecost, Eric J. and van Poeck, André (2001) *European Monetary Integration; Past, Present and Future* (Cheltenham: Edward Elgar)

Pruys, Karl Hugo (1995) *Helmut Kohl; die biographie* (Berlin: edition q)

Rasin, A. (1923) 'Financial Policy of Czechoslovakia during the First Year of its History' in J.T. Shotwell (ed.), *Economic and Social History of the World War* (Oxford: Clarendon Press)

Ross, George (1998) 'French Social Democracy and the EMU', ARENA Working Papers No. 19.

Sauzay, Brigitte and von Thadden, Rudolf (1999) *Mitterrand und die Deutschen* (Göttingen: Wallstein)

Schäuble, Wolfgang (2000) *Mitten im Leben* (Frankfurt: Bertelsmann)

Szász, André (1999) *The Road to European Monetary Union* (Basingstoke: Macmillan)

Vantoor, Wim (1997) *European Monetary Union since 1848* (Cheltenham: Edward Elgar)

Verdun, Amy (1998) 'The Role of the Delors Committee in the Creation of EMU: An Epistemic Community?', European University Institute, Working Paper RSC No. 98/44.

Wiesel, Élie (1995) *Mémoire à deux voix* (Paris: Fayard)

Woodward, Bob (2000) *Maestro: Greenspan's Fed and the American Boom* (New York: Simon & Schuster)

Woyke, Wichard (2000) *Deutsche-französische Beziehungen seit der Wiedervereinigung* (Opladen: Leske & Budrich)

Wyplosz, Charles (1997) 'EMU: Why and How It Might Happen', *Journal of Economic Perspectives*, 11(4): 3–22.

Wyplosz, Charles (1998) 'Towards a More Perfect EMU'. Paper given at symposium of Money and Credit, Madrid, November 1998.

Index

European Central Bank – *continued*
Delors Committee, 112; decision
taken October 1993 to base in
Frankfurt, 125; starts operations
(1 July, 1998), 136; early
mistakes in monetary policy, 143;
failure to ease policy sufficiently
in 2001–3, 151; dangers of
political alienation, 149–53, 167;
ECB officials mount
unconvincing defence of secrecy,
149; democratic standards should
not be left to ECB to determine
149; excessive preoccupation
with fiscal policy, 151; how
powerful is its president? 152;
how voting rights of national
central bank presidents might
change as EMU expands, 161;
proposals for reform – including
issues of transparency,
democracy, appointments, and
rotating chairmanship for big
country central bank presidents
167; how much influence can
France have on, 34; *see also*
deflation; reform proposals for
European Monetary Union;
Stability Council; lender of last
resort function
European Monetary Institute, as
foreseen by the Delors
Committee, 114; decision to base
in Frankfurt, 125; Duisenberg
refuses to become founding
president, 1993, 125; 1996 coup
in favour of Duisenberg as head,
57; Chirac decides not to
challenge coup (1996) until
Spring 1998, 130; *see also*
Lamfalussy, Alexandre
European monetary menu, the
choices available, 2–3
European Monetary System,
negotiations towards, 103; was its
birth an obstacle on the way to
monetary union? 105–6, 114;
almost breaks apart, Summer
1993, 123

European Monetary Union,
economic arguments for (as used
by Brussels), 14; undermined by
real estate cycles, 16; critical
new steps towards in late 1987
and early 1988, 109–11; blueprint
for journey towards and final
form agreed by Delors
Committee, 113; failure to delay
progress towards in wake of
German reunification imposed
high costs, 118; pressures grow to
delay, 1995–6, 130; in practice
has not provided protection
against US shocks, 146;
disappointments of experience so
far, 146–9; future expansion to
the east and north, 162; *see also*
accounting tricks; French aims in
supporting; German support for;
Hague summit (1969); Paris
declaration (1972); reform
proposals for
European political union, how Delors
committee bypassed the issue of,
112; before or after monetary
union? 51; Mitterrand and Kohl
propose an intergovernmental
conference on April 1990, 116;
absence of political union means
increased risk of monetary union
eventually falling apart or
shrinking, 139; could political
union coexist with several
currencies in Europe? 141
Évian, Franco-German summit in,
1988, 37
Exchange restrictions, abolition of a
pre-condition of progress towards
EMU, 38, 109; Delors strives to
promote legislation for
unrestricted capital flows, 108

Fabius, Laurent, ultimately rejects
idea of free float of franc in 1983,
12; his analysis of Mitterrand's
popularity, 30
Feldstein, Martin, his opposition to
European monetary union, 14